RAND ARROYO CENTER

Helping Soldiers Leverage Army Knowledge, Skills, and Abilities in Civilian Jobs

Jeffrey B. Wenger, Ellen M. Pint, Tepring Piquado, Michael G. Shanley, Trinidad Beleche, Melissa A. Bradley, Jonathan Welch, Laura Werber, Cate Yoon, Eric J. Duckworth, Nicole H. Curtis

Prepared for the United States Army
Approved for public release; distribution unlimited

For more information on this publication, visit www.rand.org/t/RR1719

Library of Congress Cataloging-in-Publication Data is available for this publication.
ISBN: 978-0-8330-9671-5

Published by the RAND Corporation, Santa Monica, Calif.

Cover photo by Staff Sgt. Joe Armas/U.S. Army

Preface

This report documents one of the primary tasks of a research project titled "Facilitating AC-to-RC and AC-to-Civilian Transitions." The overall purpose of the project was to assess the level and importance of the knowledge, skills, and abilities needed to perform in Army military occupational specialties (MOSs) to develop improved crosswalks between military and civilian occupations and to make other recommendations to improve the transition process for soldiers leaving the Regular Army.

In this report, we discuss the results of occupation surveys administered to soldiers in ten of the most populous Army MOSs, including the knowledge, skills, and abilities rated most important by soldiers in those MOSs, the best-matching civilian occupations, and comparisons with other military-civilian occupation crosswalks.

This research was sponsored by the Assistant Secretary of the Army for Manpower and Reserve Affairs and the Deputy Chief of Staff, G-1, U.S. Army, and conducted within the RAND Arroyo Center's Personnel, Training, and Health Program. RAND Arroyo Center, part of the RAND Corporation, is a federally funded research and development center sponsored by the United States Army.

The Project Unique Identification Code (PUIC) for the project that produced this document is HQD156885.

Executive Summary

As the Army reduces its end strength, the number of soldiers leaving the Regular Army has increased, raising concerns about unemployment and other transition problems for these veterans. To help improve the Army's transition assistance process, in this study we administered civilian occupation surveys to soldiers in selected Army military occupational specialties (MOSs) to assess the knowledge, skills, and abilities (KSAs) needed in these MOSs and to develop better crosswalks between military and civilian occupations. We also identified survey questions associated with soft skills, such as leadership, teamwork, and attention to detail, to assist soldiers with translating their Army experience for civilian employers.

The occupation surveys generated a rich database that can be used to characterize the KSAs needed by Army soldiers to perform their MOSs, as well as other occupation attributes, such as work activities, work context, and work style. Furthermore, the crosswalks generated from the survey responses identified both a broader range of military-civilian occupation matches and higher-quality matches than existing crosswalks. Based on these results, we recommend that the Army communicate information about these job matches to both soldiers and potential employers and that it expand use of the occupation surveys to develop crosswalks for additional MOSs.

Contents

Summary

Since 2012, the Army has reduced its active component (AC) end strength by 80,000 soldiers, and the Army plans to cut an additional 40,000 soldiers by the end of 2018. This has increased the number of soldiers leaving the Regular Army each year. Some soldiers struggle to find employment after they leave the Regular Army, and many claim unemployment compensation. Among young soldiers, unemployment was nearly 17.4 percent in 2010, and it was 15.3 percent among a comparable civilian group—suggesting that, while youth unemployment in general is a problem, young veterans have additional difficulties in the job market (Heaton and Krull, 2012). This report documents the results of a study to improve the transition process for enlisted soldiers leaving the Regular Army. As part of this study, we assessed the knowledge, skills, and abilities (KSAs) and work context, work styles, and generalized work activities of soldiers in selected military occupational specialties (MOSs) to develop improved crosswalks between military and civilian occupations and to assist soldiers with describing their work experience to potential civilian employers.

Methodology for Comparing Military and Civilian Occupations

To assess the KSAs of soldiers in ten of the most populous Army MOSs, we administered civilian occupation surveys developed by the U.S. Department of Labor to soldiers at four Army installations. This enables us to directly compare the importance and level of KSAs and job characteristics of military and civilian occupations based on the responses to each of the survey questions by soldiers and civilians. The surveys cover six domains:

- Knowledge (33 questions): sets of facts and principles needed to address problems and issues that are part of a job.
- Skills (35 questions): the abilities to perform a task well, usually developed over time through training or experience.
- Abilities (52 questions): enduring talents that can help a person do a job.
- Work Activities (41 questions): a set of similar actions that are performed together in many different jobs.
- Work Context (57 questions): work setting and its possible hazards, pace of work, and dealings with other people.
- Work Styles (16 questions): personal characteristics that can affect how well someone does a job.

Using the data generated by these surveys, we created a distance metric to identify the closest-matching civilian occupations for each of the ten MOSs. The distance metric compares the average response of the MOS to each survey question with the average response of all 761 U.S. standard civilian occupations that are surveyed by the Department of Labor. We rescaled the distance metric so that the best match across all MOSs and civilian occupations has a score of 100 and the worst match has a score of zero. For clarity in presentation, we define matches that score 80 or better as high-quality matches and present these matches in this report.[1]

To assist soldiers in translating their KSAs for civilian employers, we also identified survey questions associated with soft skills, such as leadership, teamwork, persistence, and attention to detail. Thus, the

[1] Throughout this analysis, we note that occupational matches are subject to sampling variation; that is, question responses vary depending on the soldiers and civilians who responded to the O*NET questionnaire. However, due to data limitations, we are unable to calculate standard errors for match quality. As a consequence, there may be occupational matches that are statistically equivalent to the matches presented in the analysis but despite their statistical equivalence are not included among the recommended occupations.

Table S.1
Comparison of Recommended Civilian Occupations for MOS 11B (Infantryman)

Survey Matches	Distance Metric	My Next Move for Veterans	Distance Metric
Firefighters	93	Construction laborers (E1)	64
Captains, mates, and pilots of water vessels	88	Correctional officers and jailers (E4)	76
Supervisors of fire fighting and prevention workers	86	Light truck or delivery service drivers (E4)	49
Supervisors of mechanics, installers, and repairers	84	Maintenance workers, machinery (E4)	64
Septic tank servicers and sewer pipe cleaners	83	Police and sheriff's patrol officers (E4)	80
Millwrights	82	Probation officers and correctional treatment specialists (E4)	55
Fire inspectors and investigators	82	Security guards (E4)	42
Aircraft cargo handling supervisors	81	Supervisors of correctional officers (E5)	71
Ship engineers	81	Supervisors of transportation machine and vehicle operators (E5)	79
Manufactured building and mobile home installers	80	Training and development specialists (E6)	53
Structural iron and steel workers	80	Training and development managers (E7)	56
Police and sheriff's patrol officers	80	Emergency management directors (E7)	73

NOTE: The distance metric is normalized to a scale of 0 to 100, with 100 indicating the best match.

occupation survey results also highlight the soft skills that are utilized by the MOSs we evaluated and can be cited by transitioning soldiers when communicating with potential employers.

Improving Military-Civilian Occupation Crosswalks

Based on the distance metric, we were able to identify both a broader range of civilian occupation matches and higher-quality matches for each MOS than other military-civilian crosswalks. For example, Table S.1 compares the top civilian occupation matches generated by the survey data for MOS 11B (infantryman) with those recommended by the crosswalk on the website My Next Move for Veterans. The survey matches are listed in descending order by the quality of the match, while those generated by My Next Move for Veterans are ordered by the pay grade of the transitioning soldier. Note that only one occupation, police and sheriff's patrol officers, appears on both lists. Some occupations recommended by My Next Move for Veterans, such as construction laborers, delivery service drivers, and security guards, scored very low on our distance metric, which means they do not leverage infantrymen's KSAs. This occurs, in part, because soft skills, such as leadership, teamwork, and training, coaching, and mentoring others, are less important to those occupations.

More generally, we found that some civilian occupations match well with multiple MOSs we analyzed, because they utilize KSAs common to all soldiers. However, most MOSs, especially operations support and force sustainment occupations, also have civilian occupation matches that utilize MOS-specific KSAs.

Importantly, these recommendations are based on how well an Army job matches to a select set of civilian counterparts. We note that these recommendations may not map on to soldier preferences, for at least two reasons. First, the soldier may not want to do a job that leverages the KSAs developed in the Army. Secondly, and relatedly, the soldier may not prefer particular dimensions or aspects of a job even though his or her KSAs, work context, work styles, and generalized work activities make for a good match. Hence, the soldier is simply being offered a broader choice set, and we make no inference about his or her most preferred job.

Recommendations

There are several ways the Army should make use of these data and analysis. First, the Army should provide information on the best civilian job matches to transitioning soldiers in the ten MOSs we analyzed. This information would include the types of employers they should target, the KSAs they should emphasize in their discussions with employers, and potential skill gaps they may need to overcome or credentials they may need to acquire. Although some transitioning soldiers may not be seeking civilian jobs similar to their Army MOSs, our methodology generates a broader range of civilian occupations than existing crosswalks and may help soldiers identify other options that leverage KSAs developed in the Army. Second, the Army should also develop a communication plan for employers in these occupations, identifying which MOSs are good matches for them and the KSAs these soldiers have developed in the Army. In addition, the Army should provide information to employers about the number of soldiers in these MOSs leaving the Regular Army each year and their planned geographic locations. These recommendations are limited to the MOSs for which we have sufficient data; collecting additional data for other MOSs would improve this communication plan.

Thus, we also recommend that the Army expand use of the occupation surveys to develop crosswalks for additional MOSs. The Department of Labor has already implemented online versions of the surveys to collect data on civilian occupations. Making the surveys available to soldiers online, and integrating them into the Transition Assistance Program, is one option for expanding their use that would greatly increase the amount of data available to analyze the best civilian occupation matches by MOS and pay grade. An online format could even help generate job recommendations for individual soldiers based on their own survey responses and would allow them to identify their own KSA gaps for specific careers they would like to pursue.

Acknowledgments

We thank COL Delwyn Merkerson in the Office of the Deputy Chief of Staff, G-1, U.S. Army; John Rizkallah and David Quimby in the office of the Assistant Secretary of the Army for Manpower and Reserve Affairs; and Robin Baker, the Transition Services Manager at Joint Base Lewis-McChord (JBLM), for their helpful insights and guidance throughout this project. We are also grateful to the many soldiers at JBLM and Forts Riley, Hood, and Bragg who completed occupation surveys and facilitated our visits to these installations. Their input was critical to our research.

We thank RAND colleagues Matthew Cefalu for programming and statistical advice, Carra Sims for assistance with the human subjects approval process, and Martha Friese for helping prepare this document. We also thank James Hosek of RAND and Corri Zoli of Syracuse University for their thoughtful reviews that have helped us improve this report. Finally, we thank Michael Hansen, director of the Arroyo Personnel, Training, and Health Program, for his oversight and advice on this research.

CHAPTER ONE

Introduction

Since 2012, the Army has reduced its active component (AC) end strength by 80,000 soldiers. In July 2015, it announced plans to cut an additional 40,000 soldiers by the end of fiscal year (FY) 2018 to reach a planned end strength of 450,000 (Tan, 2015). This has increased the number of enlisted soldiers leaving the Regular Army from 65,000–70,000 per year in 2006 to 2012 to about 90,000 per year since 2013.

Some soldiers struggle to find employment after they leave the Regular Army. For example, of a sample of soldiers who separated from the Army between October 2010 and December 2012, just over half made valid unemployment insurance claims within 18 months of separation.[1] Heaton and Krull (2012) find that large differences in unemployment for nonveteran and post-9/11 veteran populations are largely due demographic differences. However, for the youngest veterans (ages 18–24) unemployment remains a significant problem. In 2010, they found that even after comparing with comparable nonveterans, veteran unemployment for those 19–24 years old was two percentage points higher (17.4 veterans vs. 15.3 nonveterans). As of April of 2016, Gulf War II–era veterans had an unemployment rate of 4.1 percent, compared with an overall rate of 4.7 percent (Bureau of Labor Stat-

[1] Based on recent budget data, the Army's total costs of Unemployment Compensation for Ex-Service Members peaked at $575 million in FY 2011. In the FY 2016 President's Budget, the Army requested a total of $293 million. These figures include both soldiers leaving the Regular Army and reserve component (RC) soldiers who have been demobilized.

ics, 2016).[2] Although soldiers in some military occupational specialties (MOSs) have the knowledge, skills, and abilities (KSAs) that would appear to readily transfer to civilian jobs in comparable fields, they may lack the specific credentials or licenses they need to take full advantage of the training they received in the Army. For other MOSs, there are no clearly comparable civilian occupations. Furthermore, some soldiers may prefer civilian careers that are not related to their Army MOS.

This report documents the results of one of the primary research tasks conducted as part of a study on improving the transition process for soldiers leaving the Regular Army. We analyzed civilian occupation surveys that we administered to soldiers in ten of the Army's largest MOSs to assess the KSAs needed to perform those MOSs and to develop improved crosswalks between military and civilian occupations.[3]

Literature Review: Theory of Job Search

Active Army soldiers' pathways into the civilian job market can take many forms. One option is to return to school and attain additional degrees or certifications. Another option is to jump immediately into employment and begin searching for work. Some may combine part-time employment and schooling. For those choosing the employment path, it is important to understand the many facets of job search and the dynamics of landing a job. Labor economics has a rich and well-developed theory of job search. Standard search models (stationary models) are conceptualized as solving a search problem, where the worker chooses how much effort to put into finding a job and, based on the marketplace, the worker receives a wage offer (based on a distri-

[2] The overall figures are given in Table A-14, "Unemployed Persons by Industry and Class of Worker, Not Seasonally Adjusted" (www.bls.gov/news.release/empsit.t14.htm), and the figures for veterans are given in Table A-5, "Employment Status of the Civilian Population 18 Years and Over by Veteran Status, Period of Service, and Sex, Not Seasonally Adjusted" (www.bls.gov/news.release/empsit.t05.htm). Note that both rates are "not seasonally adjusted."

[3] We initially targeted the 20 largest MOSs in the Army, but only obtained sufficient sample sizes to analyze ten MOSs.

bution of wage offers) and a frequency of offers based on a wage-offer arrival rate. Both of these market attributes are thought of as constant over time. The job seeker chooses to accept the job if the offer wage is above his or her "reservation wage"—the lowest wage for which he or she would accept employment. These initial models implied that reservation wages are constant over the spell of unemployment (J. McCall, 1970; Mortenson, 1970).

It is important to note that the reservation wage is one of the few factors that the job seeker has control over—that and search effort. Consequently, the reservation wage has been the subject of much research, because it is the key determinant in whether a person becomes employed. It should not be surprising that empirical evidence did not support the theory that reservation wages remained constant over the spell of unemployment. In general, the literature suggests that reservation wages decline with the duration of unemployment (Kasper, 1967; Sant, 1977; Kiefer and Neumann, 1979)—that is, job-seekers become willing to accept lower wages as their duration of unemployment increases. Most research in this vein allows for nonstationarity (job conditions and job search change over the spell of unemployment). This work suggests that falling reservation wages can arise from finite worker lifetimes (Gronau, 1971), liquidity constraints (Danforth, 1979; Mortenson, 1986; Wolpin, 1987), the depletion of unemployment benefits (Mortenson, 1977; Burdett, 1979), a declining job offer arrival rate over time (Burdett and Mortenson, 1980), a declining mean or variance of the wage offer distribution (Lippman and J. McCall, 1976; Mortenson, 1986), and systematic rather than purely random search (Salop, 1973).

Other research provides insights into why the reservation wage might exhibit a nonconstant time profile. Burdett and Vishwanath (1988) show that the ability of workers to learn about the wage distribution through continued search can cause the reservation wage to decline over time. Van den Berg (1990) shows that the reservation wage is strictly decreasing over time if unemployment insurance benefits are decreasing, the arrival rate of job offers is decreasing, or the wage offer distribution at each point in time first-order stochastically dominates (i.e., has higher mean than) or is a mean-preserving spread of (i.e., has higher variance than) the wage distributions that exist at all later points in time. In contrast, B. McCall (1994) shows that if workers search among jobs that are heterogeneous in their inspection match or experience match uncertainty, reservation wages can be constant or even increase with time.

The empirical literature on job search has several important strands that have focused on different dimensions of job search: the wage offer arrival rate, the mean or variance of the offer distribution, the reservation wage, search costs, and discount rates (Flinn and Heckman, 1982; Wolpin, 1987; Stern, 1989; Blackaby et al., 2007). Other studies focus on the impacts of wealth (Bloemen and Stancanelli, 2001), previous wages (Hogan, 2004), demographics such as age, race, gender, or education (Holzer, 1986; Petterson, 1997, 1998), health (Brown, Roberts, and Taylor, 2010), search costs (Jones, 1989), local economic conditions (Haurin and Sridhar, 2003), labor market scale (Petrongolo and Pissarides, 2006), or social assistance payments (Alexopoulos and Gladden, 2004; Mitra, 2007; Gorter and Gorter, 1993; Della Vigna and Paserman, 2005).

Drawing on this prior research, the most salient issues for soldiers are probably search effort and learning models of job search, where job-seekers are both learning about how to systematize their search (Salop, 1973) and learning about the wage distribution (Burdett and Vishwanath, 1988). Both of these types of learning reduce the reservation wage over the spell of unemployment. B. McCall (1994), however, shows that uncertainty about match quality may lead to increases in the reservation wage. Increases in the reservation wage are likely to lead to prolonged spells of unemployment. By providing better information to soldiers about the potential match quality, we may militate against prolonged spells of unemployment by reducing this source of uncertainty.

Outline of Report

Chapter Two describes our methodology for creating improved military-civilian occupation crosswalks, including a discussion of the occupation surveys we used to assess the KSAs of soldiers. Chapter Three presents the results of this analysis, including the highest-rated KSAs and other job characteristics of ten of the largest Army MOSs, recommended civilian occupations for each MOS, and a comparison with the occupations recommended by My Next Move for Veterans, one of the existing military-civilian occupation crosswalks. Chapter Four then generalizes findings about civilian occupations that match to multiple MOSs. Chapter Five concludes with a summary of our findings and recommendations.

CHAPTER TWO

A Methodology for Comparing Military and Civilian Occupations

In this chapter, we describe the methodology for our analysis of the KSAs needed to perform Army MOSs. This analysis is based on the surveys used by the U.S. Department of Labor to classify civilian occupations, which we administered to soldiers in the 20 largest MOSs at four Army installations. For ten of these MOSs in which we obtained a sufficient sample size, we can compare the responses to each question with those of a wide array of civilian occupations to identify which are the "closest" matches with each MOS. This comparison does not necessarily examine the specific technical skills associated with Army MOSs, such as weapon proficiency, logistical management, and emergency medical care, and match those with civilian occupations. Rather, we evaluate how military jobs compare with civilian jobs in terms of KSAs, work styles, work context, and work activities, which include a wide range of both technical and nontechnical attributes of workers and occupations. We also quantify the differences and document *how* jobs in the military and civilian sectors differ. Thus, we believe our methodology is a more comprehensive approach to comparing military and civilian occupations than is used to build existing crosswalks.

To assist soldiers in translating their KSAs for civilian employers, we also developed a definition of soft skills based on Hardison et al. (2015) and identified survey questions related to these skills (see Appendix A). In contrast to technical skills, Hardison et al. define soft skills as essential nontechnical skills (e.g., leadership, team work, persistence, and attention to detail) that veterans offer employers and that are not tied to specific occupations. Many military-civilian job translators, which have been in development since the early 1980s, are only beginning to incorporate soft skills in constructing their crosswalks. As a result, civilian employers tend to have difficulty understanding the soft skills that veterans possess, and veterans have difficulty identifying and explaining them in the context of job interviews and résumés.[1]

In this chapter, we provide some additional information on the U.S. Department of Labor's Occupational Information Network (O*NET) program, which developed the surveys and collects and analyzes data on civilian occupations. We then discuss our implementation of the surveys and describe the distance metric we created to compare Army MOSs with civilian occupations. In the next chapter, we present the results of our analysis for each MOS.

Background on O*NET

The O*NET program is the most systematic and extensive source for information about civilian occupations in the United States. A central component of the O*NET program is the O*NET database, which contains information on hundreds of occupations. Starting in 1998, O*NET has collected information about both workers' KSAs in their respective occupations and the job characteristics or job dimensions associated with performing those occupations (Mariani, 1999). O*NET data are gathered by surveying a broad range of workers from each occupation. Because the U.S. labor market is ever-changing, the data are continually updated. As occupations evolve, new occupations are created, or old occupations become obsolete, current information about each occupation is incorporated into the O*NET database.

The O*NET database consists of a series of modules grouped into six content areas, as shown in Table 2.1. Three of the content areas focus on the characteristics of workers in each occupation, and three content areas focus on characteristics of the occupation. Generally, worker characteristics include KSAs and qualifications, whereas job

[1] For additional discussion of this point, see Hardison et al. (2015).

Table 2.1
O*NET Modules and Content Areas

Worker-Oriented Modules	Job-Oriented Modules
1. Worker Characteristics Abilities* Occupational interests Work values Work styles*	4. Occupational Requirements Work activities* Organizational context Work context*
2. Worker Requirements Skills* Knowledge* Education	5. Workforce Characteristics Labor market information Occupational outlook
3. Experience Requirements Education and training * Basic skills – entry requirements Cross functional skills – entry requirements Licensing	6. Occupation-Specific Information Tasks Tools Technology

SOURCE: O*NET Resource Center (undated).

* Indicates module was administered to Army enlisted personnel.

characteristics include work activities, organizational and work context, tasks and technology, and labor market information. The survey modules we administered to soldiers are indicated in Table 2.1 by an asterisk. Most of the remaining modules are not survey-based or must be tailored to each occupation. In particular, the task lists, technology, and tools, as well as the status of the labor market for a particular occupation, fall into this category.[2] As a consequence, those modules are not used in this analysis.

Each of the survey modules contains a series of questions related to the attributes of either the worker or the job. For example, one of the worker characteristics modules collects information using a series of questions about a worker's abilities. O*NET defines abilities as "enduring attributes of the individual that influence performance." Additional abilities are further subdivided into cognitive abilities, psycho-

[2] As part of this study, we experimented with the design and implementation of task lists for two Army MOSs, 11B (Infantryman) and 19K (M1 armor crewman). The results of this effort are described in Appendix B.

motor abilities, physical abilities, and sensory abilities. In all, there are 52 abilities questions.

For respondents to more easily understand and answer questions in the abilities module, each O*NET question is defined. For example, a question on "arm-hand steadiness" is defined as "[t]he ability to keep your hand and arm steady while moving your arm or while holding your arm and hand in one position." Respondents are asked two questions about this ability. First, "How important is the ability to your current job?" rated on a 5-point scale: 1 "not important," 2 "somewhat important," 3 "important," 4 "very important," and 5 "extremely important." If respondents rate the importance of the ability at two or higher, they are then asked, "What level of the ability is needed to perform your current job?" Levels range from 1 to 7, with 1 indicating that a low level of ability is necessary and 7 indicating that an extremely high level is necessary. Importantly, each level question has three anchors to help respondents understand how to rate their job on this scale. In the "arm-hand steadiness" question, the anchors indicate that 2 is equivalent to "light a candle," 4 is "thread a needle," and 6 is "cut facets in a diamond." Most often, the anchors are located at scale values 2, 4 and 6, and the respondent is left to infer the meaning of 1, 3, 5 and 7; however, the anchors are sometimes provided at other points on the scale.

There are four modules of the database that follow this format:

- Knowledge (33 questions): sets of facts and principles needed to address problems and issues that are part of a job.
- Skills (35 questions): the abilities to perform tasks well, usually developed over time through training or experience.
- Abilities (52 questions): enduring talents that can help a person do a job.
- Work Activities (41 questions): a set of similar actions that are performed together in many different jobs.

In the remaining two survey modules, a single question is asked on a 5-point scale. In the "Work Context" questionnaire, respondents are asked about their working conditions—ranging from work setting and its possible hazards, the pace of work, and dealings with other people to the frequency of particular activities. All questions are on a 5-point scale and responses are typically framed as frequency—how often does the respondent engage in that activity (never [1] to always [5])—or importance (not important at all [1] to extremely important [5]).

There are two survey modules that follow this format:

- Work Context (57 questions): work setting and its possible hazards, pace of work, and dealings with other people.
- Work Styles (16 questions): personal characteristics that can affect how well someone does a job.

In all, there are 161 questions that require a two-part response (importance and level) and an additional 73 questions that require a single response on a 5-point scale. Taken together, the O*NET modules that we selected for use in this study have 234 questions about both the attributes of the worker doing the job and attributes of the job itself.

Sprinkled throughout each of the survey modules are questions that relate to soft skills, as defined by Hardison et al. (2015). For example, the skills survey asks about "critical thinking," and the knowledge survey asks about "education and training," including curriculum and training design and instruction of individuals and groups. The work activities survey includes questions about experience "developing and building teams" and "coaching and developing others." The work style survey asks about "leadership," "adaptability and flexibility," and "stress tolerance." Using a methodology described in Appendix A, we identified questions associated with soft skills in each of the survey modules. In our analysis, we flag these attributes and highlight them in our descriptions of Army MOSs and our comparisons of military and civilian occupations.[3] In all, we defined 25 percent of the survey questions to be directly associated with soft skills.

---

[3] Appendix A identifies and defines 18 underlying soft skills used in Army MOSs, associating specific questions in the O*NET surveys to each one.

The O*NET survey instruments are designed to be self-contained, with all definitions provided, and targeted at respondents with at least an eighth-grade reading level. Since, with few exceptions, soldiers are high school graduates, administering the surveys should pose no problems with comprehension or readability.[4] In practice, soldiers expressed no difficulty answering the questions, and most completed the questionnaires in 20–40 minutes, depending on the number of questions in their survey packet.

Some concerns about the applicability and usefulness of the O*NET system for conducting Army occupational analysis could remain, considering that it was designed to evaluate civilian occupations. However, prior research by Russell, Mumford, and Peterson (1996, as quoted by Russell et al., 2008) suggests that senior noncommissioned officers were able to reliably rate the occupations they examined using O*NET survey modules (M1 armor crewman [19K], signal support systems specialist [25U], military police [31B], and motor transport operator [88M]).[5] In general, Russell et al. found evidence that (1) Army occupations were reliably rated using the O*NET rating scales, (2) O*NET rating scales were able to differentiate Army occupations, and (3) noncommissioned officers who were subject-matter experts were able to rate jobs similarly to job analysts and were found to be statistically comparable to civilian expert analysts. Overall, the study found that "an Army-specific occupational analysis system is practicable using O*NET descriptors as a foundation" (Russell et al., 2008, p. viii).

---

[4] We elected to administer the surveys in person to groups of soldiers at Army installations in case there were any difficulties in interpreting the O*NET questions. Given that we did not find any problems with interpretation, it should be feasible to implement the surveys online if the Army wants to extend the analysis to additional MOSs.

[5] The noncommissioned officers were asked to rate an entry-level soldier (skill level 10) in the MOS.

Implementation of O*NET Surveys

Starting in March 2015, we implemented the O*NET survey modules identified in Table 2.1 to Regular Army enlisted personnel at four installations: Joint Base Lewis-McChord (JBLM), Fort Riley, Fort Hood, and Fort Bragg. The research team initially targeted the 20 most-populous Army MOSs for data collection in an effort to cover as many transitioning soldiers as possible. In practice, our response rate was limited by the number of soldiers that units were able to excuse from their duties to attend our survey sessions, which were held in classrooms on the installations, and the units sometimes sent soldiers whose MOSs were not among the 20 largest. In Table 2.2, we show the results of our surveys by MOS group and installation. Survey response rates for each MOS are shown in Appendix C.

The survey instruments are identical to those administered by O*NET and can be found online at https://www.onetcenter.org/questionnaires.html (O*NET Resource Center, undated).[6] Because the combined surveys are quite long (234 items, with 161 items having a two-part answer—importance and level), we followed O*NET's practice of grouping the survey modules into five packets and administered each packet separately to soldiers. The packets contained all of the

Table 2.2
Number of Surveys Collected by Army Installation

	Total		Used in Analysis	
Location	**Count**	**Percentage**	**Count**	**Percentage**
Ft. Bragg	308	25.08	191	23.10
Ft. Hood	313	25.49	244	29.50
JBLM	301	24.51	179	21.64
Ft. Riley	306	24.92	213	25.76
Total	1,228	100	827	100

[6] We adapted O*NET's cover page of background questions (including demographic information and time in current occupation) to fit the Army context.

questions from the six modules, with knowledge and work styles questions combined into a single packet.[7] In keeping with O*NET guidelines, our goal was to administer at least eight surveys of each of the five packets to soldiers in each of the targeted MOSs. This means that at least 40 soldiers had to complete the O*NET questionnaire in each targeted MOS in order to have a sufficient sample size to be included in our occupation analysis.[8]

For MOS 11B (Infantryman), this goal was not difficult to meet, since it is the most populous MOS in the Army, accounting for about 11 percent of Regular Army soldiers. Other MOSs with a sufficient sample size for analysis were 12B (combat engineer), 13B (cannon crewmember), 19D (cavalry scout), 19K (M1 armor crewman), 31B (military police), 35F (intelligence analyst), 68W (health care specialist), 91B (wheeled vehicle mechanic), and 92Y (unit supply specialist). These MOSs account for about 40 percent of the AC enlisted force. We were not able to obtain a sufficient sample size to analyze the remaining ten targeted MOSs.[9]

As Table 2.2 indicates, we administered surveys to a total of 1,228 soldiers at the four installations, but we were able to use only 827 in the analysis due to insufficient sample sizes in some MOSs.[10] Given the high density of MOS 11B (infantryman), we had significantly more 11B responses (178 total survey packets) than we did for any other MOS. This allowed us to conduct a number of sensitivity tests, such as

---

[7] This packet also includes four questions on education and training requirements for the occupation.

[8] We administered the Abilities survey to soldiers in pay grades E7 to E9, who have supervisory roles over more junior soldiers, because O*NET uses occupational analysts rather than job incumbents to complete these questions. This constraint proved to be the most difficult hurdle for some of the targeted MOSs. (See survey counts in Appendix C.)

[9] These MOSs were 11C (indirect fire infantryman), 13F (fire support specialist), 25B (information technology specialist), 25U (signal support systems specialist), 42A (human resources specialist), 74D (chemical, biological, radiological, and nuclear specialist), 88M (motor transport operator), 92A (automated logistical specialist), 92F (petroleum supply specialist), and 92G (food service specialist). They account for about 20 percent of the AC enlisted force.

[10] There were a number of additional MOSs with nearly enough surveys to conduct the analysis. Future research may be able to utilize this information if the Army pursues a more complete occupational crosswalk analysis.

whether soldiers in higher pay grades responded differently than more-junior soldiers.[11] In practice, we did not find any significant differences among various subgroups of soldiers, so our results are reported for the MOS as a whole.

We also used Fleiss's kappa to calculate inter-rater reliability for survey respondents by MOS. For seven of the ten MOSs, there was "fair" agreement, on average, across the six survey modules, while the remaining three showed "slight" agreement. While these ratings are relatively low, they reflect heterogeneity among pay grade, work assignments, and other factors within an MOS. With additional survey observations, it might be possible to improve inter-rater reliability among subgroups within an MOS, and also to generate better military-civilian occupation crosswalks for these subgroups. More details on our reliability assessment are provided in Appendix C.

Distance Metric

By administering the O*NET surveys without modification to soldiers in the most-populous MOSs, we are able to make direct comparisons with civilian occupations. We accomplish this by way of a "distance metric." The distance metric is a formula that calculates the difference between the average score of the MOS to *each* O*NET question or attribute and the average score of *every other* occupation in the civilian sector. Based on the survey responses, we can compare an MOS with *every* civilian occupation at the six-digit standard occupation classification (SOC) level included in the O*NET data collection program, or a total of 761 different civilian occupations. This includes, for example, such disparate occupations as firefighters, pipefitters, fashion models, and computer programmers. For each of these comparisons, we calculate a score, or distance metric, that tells us how similar (or different) each civilian occupation is to that MOS.

---

[11] Since the abilities survey module was only given to pay grades E7–E9, the sensitivity tests were not conducted on this module.

Consider the following simplified example: There are three attributes that describe a job—critical thinking, trunk strength, and attention to detail. In this example, there is a single response to each survey question, which is simply an importance measure that ranges from 1 "not important" to 5 "extremely important." We survey soldiers in a single MOSs and calculate their average responses to each of these survey questions. Then we can simply compare the average responses from this Army MOS with those for two civilian occupations in the O*NET database. For example, the average responses for MOS 11B, firefighters, and construction laborers are shown in Table 2.3.

In this example, we square the difference between the average responses for MOS 11B and the civilian occupations on each attribute, and then sum the squares. The best possible score on this metric is zero, which would occur if all of the average responses were identical. Conversely, if the responses are exactly opposite to each other (for each item that soldiers indicated was "extremely important," the civilian occupation indicated that it was "not important at all," or vice versa), the differences between the scores would be 5 – 1 = 4 or 1 – 5 = –4,

Table 2.3
Simplified Example of Occupation Distance Metric

Attribute	MOS 11B Avergage (A)	Civilian Occupation Average (B)	(A – B) (Difference)	$(A - B)^2$ (Difference Squared)
Firefighter				
Critical thinking	4.25	3.56	0.69	0.48
Trunk strength	4.46	3.57	0.89	0.79
Attention to detail	4.81	4.19	0.62	0.38
			Total score:	1.65
Construction laborer				
Critical thinking	4.25	2.88	1.37	1.88
Trunk strength	4.46	3.12	1.34	1.80
Attention to detail	4.81	4.04	0.77	0.59
			Total score:	4.27

and the squared differences would be 16 for each. Since there are three attributes, we get $3 \times 16 = 48$ as the worst possible score. Thus, in this example, the best match for MOS 11B would be the civilian occupation with the total score closest to zero. Based on this simplified distance metric, firefighter is a better match for MOS 11B than construction laborer, because the sum of the squared differences in average responses to the three questions is smaller.

In practice, our formula is somewhat more complicated, because there are 234 job attributes to compare across military and civilian occupations. We also wanted to weight each O*NET attribute equally, because we have no *a priori* reason to believe that some attributes are more important than others. For 161 attributes, O*NET provides measures of both the importance and level of the attribute, and we use the following formula to sum the distance metrics for each individual question:

$$\sum_{n=1}^{161} Distance = (MOS - Civ)_{IM}^2 + \\ (|MOS_{IM} \times MOS_{LV} - Civ_{IM} \times Civ_{LV}|) + \\ (MOS - Civ)_{LV}^2$$

where *IM* stands for the importance measure from the O*NET question and *LV* stands for the difficulty level. The vertical bars represent the absolute value of the difference, so that each component of this distance metric is positive. Note that since importance is rated on a scale from 1 to 5 and level is rated from 0 to 7, the maximum distance for each individual question is 100. We use the product in the equation above because it better captures the positive correlation in the responses than does a simple summation of importance and level. However, experimentation with alternate functional forms of the metric did not result in significant changes in our recommended occupational matches. For instance, eliminating the importance and level interaction from the formula still matched 11B to firefighters as our best match.

For the 73 O*NET attributes that are measured on a single 5-point scale, we use the following formula to sum the distance metrics:

$$\sum_{n=1}^{73} Distance = |MOS - Civ| \times 25.$$

In this case, we multiply the absolute value by 25 so that the maximum distance for each individual question is 100. Using these distance metrics, the total distance between two occupations could potentially range from 0 to 23,400.[12] For ease of interpretation, we rescale our total distance metric such that the best match between any two military and civilian occupations is 100 and the worst match is 0.

Standard Errors

Ideally, we would have sufficient number of survey responses in each MOS to calculate a standard error for the distance metric. Unfortunately, for many MOSs, we had only eight complete responses for the O*NET questionnaire (this is similar to civilian O*NET reporting). Consequently, our Monte Carlo estimates of the standard errors are quite large. Even for MOS 11B (infantrymen), where we had 33 completed surveys (see Appendix C, Table C.1), standard errors were quite large. This is due to the fact that the standard error of the distance metric is determined by both the standard error of the military responses and the standard error of the civilian responses. We do not have access to the microdata for the civilian sector; consequently, our Monte Carlo estimates assume zero variance for civilian O*NET responses, resulting in a smaller error variance estimate. Despite this, our Monte Carlo estimates suggest that there may be occupational matches that are statistically equivalent to the matches presented in the analysis. While some matches are statistically equivalent, they are not included among the recommended occupations. **This implies that future analysis—that includes new soldier responses to the O*NET questionnaire—may result in slightly different sets of recommendations.**

---

[12] We experimented with some variations in the calculation of the distance metric, but found that these variations did not have much effect on the ranking of matches between military and civilian occupations.

Not being able to discern the recommended occupations from those that are statistically similar (but not recommended) would be eliminated once we collect estimates of O*NET attributes on a large sample of military occupations providing for accurate estimates of the standard error of the distance metric. That is, once we have a precise estimate of the MOS attributes via the O*NET questionnaire, we will be able to discern which occupations are statistically equivalent in match quality.

Evaluation of Occupation Matches

We used the distance metric to compare the average survey responses of the ten MOSs for which we had sufficient data with the average responses of every six-digit civilian occupation in the O*NET database. This process generates a 1 to N ranking of civilian occupations from the closest to the farthest from each MOS. However, depending on the responses to the O*NET survey questions, some MOSs have a larger number of closely matching civilian occupations than other MOSs. We decided to use a cut-off point of 80 on the rescaled distance metric to define a "high-quality" match between military and civilian occupations. Approximately 14 percent of all civilian occupation comparisons across the ten MOSs meet this criterion (i.e., they score 80 or higher on the distance metric).

We also found that some civilian occupations appeared frequently among the highest-ranking matches for several MOSs, while other occupation matches were unique to specific MOSs. Therefore, we decided to categorize civilian occupations that matched with four or more of the ten MOSs we analyzed as "general matches" and the remainder as "MOS-specific matches."[13] Table 2.4 summarizes the number of civilian occupation matches for each MOS that scored 80 or higher on our scale of 0 to 100. Note that infantrymen (MOS 11B) and M1 armor crewmen (19K) have the fewest number of high-quality matches and they are all classified as general matches. Conversely, unit

[13] In Appendix D, Table D.1, we list all 66 of the civilian occupations that we classify as general matches.

Table 2.4
Number of High Quality Civilian Occupation Matches for Each MOS

MOS	Description	Number of High-Quality Matches	Number of High-Quality Matches with Education < Bachelor's Degree	Number of General Matches	Number of MOS-Specific Matches
11B	Infantryman	13	12	12	0
12B	Combat engineer	92	78	60	18
13B	Cannon crewmember	48	48	41	7
19D	Cavalry scout	70	68	55	13
19K	M1 armor crewman	13	13	13	0
31B	Military police	46	33	30	3
35F	Intelligence analyst	256	53	23	30
68W	Health care specialist	54	41	35	6
91B	Wheeled vehicle repairer	95	93	50	43
92Y	Unit supply specialist	363	181	49	132

NOTES: The last two columns show general and MOS-specific matches requiring less than a bachelor's degree at entry. Matches do not account for statistically similar occupational matches resulting from estimation variance.

supply specialists (92Y) and intelligence analysts (35F) have a very large number of high-quality matches, as do wheeled vehicle repairers (91B) and combat engineers (12B).

Some civilian occupations that are high-quality matches on the distance metric are less promising for enlisted personnel than others. For example, they may require education, work experience, or credentials that soldiers are not likely to have, they may pay relatively low wages, or there may be relatively few such jobs in the U.S. economy. For example, in the fourth column of Table 2.4, we screen out jobs that require a bachelor's degree or more education at entry. The remaining jobs may still require an associate's degree or postsecondary certification, but these qualifications may be within reach if a soldier can invest in some short-term training or education. This additional criterion reduces the number of high-quality matches for most of the MOSs we analyzed. Nevertheless, there is still a wide range of high-quality civilian job matches available to most MOSs. In particular, unit supply specialists (92Y) appear to have KSAs that are applicable to a large number of civilian jobs.

In Chapter Three, we describe the results of our occupation survey analysis for each of the ten MOSs for which we have sufficient data. For MOSs that have large numbers of high-quality matching civilian occupations, we list the top ten general and MOS-specific matches that require less than a bachelor's degree at entry. We define the top ten matches based on the sum of their rankings on the distance metric, median wages, and prevalence of the occupation in the U.S. economy, in order to focus on the most promising matches for transitioning soldiers.

In Chapter Four, we explore the common factors that lead to general matches between civilian occupations and the Army MOSs we analyzed.

CHAPTER THREE

Improving Military-Civilian Occupation Crosswalks

In this chapter, we discuss the results of our analysis for each of the ten MOSs with sufficient data. For each MOS, we discuss the top-ranking KSAs and work attributes based on soldiers' survey responses, the best-matching civilian occupations, and a comparison of our results with the occupations recommended by My Next Move for Veterans.

In defining the best-matching civilian occupations, we first focus on "high-quality" matches, i.e., those that scored 80 or higher (on a scale of 0 to 100) on our distance metric. We present information on three additional criteria that may be relevant to transitioning soldiers: prevalence of the occupation in the U.S. economy, median pay in the occupation, and education required at entry. These criteria increase emphasis on civilian occupations that are more likely to have openings for transitioning soldiers and those that pay relatively well. We also focus on occupations that require no more than a postsecondary certification or an associate's degree at entry.

To illustrate our methodology, we first describe our results for MOS 11B (infantryman) in detail. The remaining sections of this chapter summarize our results for each of the other nine MOSs we analyzed.

Occupation Analysis for Infantryman (MOS 11B)

Based on the Army's description of MOS 11B, the primary tasks of infantrymen are to supervise, lead, or serve as a member of an infantry activity that employs individual small arms weapons or heavy anti-armor crew served weapons, either from a vehicle or dismounted, in support of offensive and defensive combat operations. Infantrymen are able to navigate mounted or dismounted using a map, conduct operations in day and night and varying terrain, and perform as a member of a team. Infantrymen communicate to higher headquarters and teammates through secure radio, use hand and arm signals, and are able to identify the enemy and call for indirect fire support. Additionally, infantrymen conduct battle damage assessment and reports (Department of the Army, 2008a).

These tasks may not sound similar to many civilian occupations, but using the O*NET surveys, we are able to identify a broader range of MOS attributes that are directly comparable with civilian occupations.

Top-Rated KSAs for Infantrymen

Table 3.1 shows the KSAs that the sample of MOS 11B soldiers rated the highest, with soft skills shown in shaded cells. These attributes are measured with two-part questions; importance is rated on a 5-point scale and level is rated on a 7-point scale. The score is calculated as the product of these two values. The top-rated knowledge and skill areas include some soft skills related to training others and critical thinking, whereas the top-rated abilities are all classified by O*NET as physical or sensory abilities.

Table 3.2 shows the remaining top-rated occupation attributes, work activities, work context, and work styles, with soft skills shown in shaded cells. The score for work activities is calculated as the product of the average importance and level scores for infantrymen; work context and work styles are both scored on a scale of 1 to 5. In contrast to the results for KSAs, two-thirds of the top-rated work attributes are associated with soft skills, including decisionmaking, teamwork, training others, oral communication, and handling work stress.

Table 3.1
Top-Rated KSAs for MOS 11B

Knowledge	Skills	Abilities
Public safety and security (17.4)	Equipment maintenance (20.8)	Far vision (29.2)
Geography (17.1)	Instructing (20.1)	Night vision (27.7)
Education and training (15.4)	Critical thinking (20.0)	Depth perception (25.9)
Mechanical (13.5)	Time management (19.6)	Peripheral vision (25.8)
Administration and management (13.3)	Active listening (19.1)	Stamina (27.9)
		Trunk strength (27.1)
		Explosive strength (26.8)
		Static strength (26.5)
		Reaction time (27.0)
		Sound localization (26.3)

NOTES: Score in parentheses is the product of the average importance score (scale of 1 to 5) and average level score (scale of 1 to 7). Soft skills are shown in shaded cells.

Table 3.2
Top-Rated Work Attributes for MOS 11B

Work Activities	Work Context	Work Styles
Performing general physical activities (27.8)	Contact with others (4.9)	Stress tolerance (4.8)
Making decisions and solving problems (22.0)	Work with work group or team (4.8)	Attention to detail (4.8)
Communicating with supervisors, peers, or subordinates (21.6)	Face-to-face discussions (4.7)	Adaptability/flexibility (4.7)
Coaching and developing others (21.1)	Outdoors, exposed to weather (4.5)	Dependability (4.7)
Handling and moving objects (21.0)	Time pressure (4.5)	Integrity (4.7)

NOTES: For work activities, score in parentheses is the product of the average importance score (scale of 1 to 5) and level score (scale of 1 to 7); for work context and work styles, score in parentheses is on a scale of 1 to 5. Soft skills are shown in shaded cells.

Best-Matching Civilian Occupations for Infantrymen

As we discussed in Chapter Two, we use the survey responses to calculate a distance metric for each of the ten Army MOSs to 761 detailed occupations from the SOC system—each occupation has an O*NET database of survey scores associated with it. Thus, we are able to compare the responses of soldiers in Army MOSs with the responses of civilian job incumbents to see how jobs differ from the military to the civilian sector. Since we have ten MOSs and 761 SOC codes with matched O*NET data, our calculations generate a database of 7,610 distance scores. Because the raw distance metrics are difficult to interpret, we rescale all of the scores so that they range from 100 (best match) to 0 (worst match).

A score of zero indicates that the civilian occupation had the largest observed distance between it and the Army MOS. For instance, a fashion model was the civilian occupation with the furthest distance (i.e., worst match) from MOS 11B. Using the same scale, a firefighter was the best match with MOS 11B, with a score of 93. For brevity of presentation, we define a high-quality match as one that scores an 80 or higher on our 100-point scale. Based on the distribution of all 7,610 distance scores, an 80 corresponds to a B (approximately the 86th percentile of the distribution). We put all ten MOSs on the same 0–100 scale so that we can compare the quality of matches across MOSs. This will allow us to say, for example, whether a firefighter is a better match for an infantryman (11B) or a combat engineer (12B).

Table 3.3 shows the 12 high-quality civilian occupation matches for infantrymen, along with the prevalence of each occupation in the U.S. economy, median wages, and education required at entry. As we extended our occupational analysis to additional MOSs, we found that all of these occupations matched well with four or more of the ten MOSs we analyzed. Therefore, in the remaining sections, we distinguish between general matches and MOS-specific matches. We describe the set of 66 total occupations that we classify as general matches in Chapter Four.

Next, we consider in more detail why firefighter is the closest-matching civilian occupation for infantryman. The survey data allow us to investigate, in depth, the specific attributes that both firefighters

Table 3.3
12 High-Quality Civilian Occupation Matches for Infantrymen (MOS 11B)

Civilian Occupation	Number of U.S. Jobs	Median Wages	Education at Entry	Distance Metric
Firefighters	308,790	$45,970	High school diploma	93
Captains, mates, and pilots of water vessels	30,690	$72,340	Postsecondary certification	88
First-line supervisors of fire fighting and prevention workers	59,870	$70,670	High school diploma	86
First-line supervisors of mechanics, installers, and repairers	434,810	$62,150	High school diploma	84
Septic tank servicers and sewer pipe cleaners	24,350	$34,810	Less than high school	83
Millwrights	39,290	$50,460	High school diploma	82
Fire inspectors and investigators	11,370	$56,130	Some college	82
Aircraft cargo handling supervisors	5,750	$47,760	High school diploma	81
Ship engineers	10,060	$68,100	Postsecondary certification	81
Structural iron and steel workers	60,010	$48,200	High school diploma	80
Manufactured building and mobile home installers	3,280	$29,600	Less than high school	80
Police and sheriff's patrol officers	638,810	$56,810	High school diploma	80

and infantrymen listed as important to their jobs. Table 3.4 shows firefighters' top-rated occupation attributes from each survey module. The number in parentheses after each attribute shows how infantrymen (MOS 11B) ranked those attributes, with soft skills shown in shaded cells. For example, customer and personal service is the knowledge attribute ranked highest by firefighters, but it is ranked 15th out of 33

Table 3.4
Top-Rated Occupation Attributes for Firefighters and Infantrymen's Ratings of Those Attributes

Knowledge (33 Questions)	Skills (35 Questions)	Abilities (52 Questions)
Customer and personal service (15)	Coordination (7)	Problem sensitivity (20)
Public safety and security (1)	Monitoring (11)	Reaction time (5)
Education and training (3)	Active listening (5)	Oral comprehension (34)
Mechanical (4)	Critical thinking (3)	Static strength (7)
Geography (2)	Speaking (8)	Multi-limb coordination (43)
		Oral expression (30)
		Manual dexterity (18)
		Trunk strength (4)

Work Activities (41 Questions)	Work Context (57 Questions)	Work Styles (16 Questions)
Performing general physical activities (1)	Wear common protective or safety equipment (12)	Dependability (4)
Handling and moving objects (5)	In an enclosed vehicle or equipment (19)	Cooperation (8)
Operating vehicles, mechanized devices, or equipment (9)	Face-to-face discussions (3)	Stress tolerance (1)
Monitor processes, materials, or surroundings (17)	Freedom to make decisions (34)	Self-control (6)
Making decisions and solving problems (2)	Responsible for others' health and safety (8)	Integrity (5)
	Work with work group or team (2)	
	Outdoors, exposed to weather (4)	
	Impact of decisions on co-workers or company results (20)	

NOTES: Attributes are listed in the order they are ranked by firefighters. Rankings by infantrymen are shown in parentheses. Soft skills are shown in shaded cells.

knowledge attributes by infantrymen. As Table 3.4 indicates, many of the firefighters' top-rated attributes were also rated in the top ten by infantrymen. There are particularly strong overlaps in knowledge, work activities, and work styles, with three or four of the firefighters' top five attributes also rated in the top five by infantrymen. We can also use the survey results to identify potential skill gaps, i.e., attributes that are rated highly by firefighters, but not by infantrymen, such as oral comprehension, oral expression, multi-limb coordination, and freedom to make decisions.

It appears that infantrymen and firefighters are a good match because of the overlap between their KSAs and work attributes, including both soft skills, such as teamwork, communications, critical thinking, dependability, and stress tolerance, and the physical requirements of the jobs, such as strength, reaction time, handling and moving objects, and working outdoors.

Comparison of Survey Matches for Infantrymen with My Next Move for Veterans

Next, we compare the matches derived from the occupation surveys with the civilian occupations recommended by My Next Move for Veterans, a commonly used military-civilian occupation crosswalk developed by O*NET for the U.S. Department of Labor.[1] My Next Move for Veterans is designed for U.S. veterans currently looking for jobs. Using this website, veterans can search for careers based on keywords, by browsing industries that employ different types of workers, or by entering their military occupation code. This is one of the more highly developed crosswalks available to veterans; it is based on an analysis of military and civilian occupational data (e.g., comparisons of job duties or tasks) and supplemented with expert opinion.

To compare the occupations recommended by My Next Move for Veterans with those we derived from the occupation survey results, we calculated the distance metric for those occupations. Table 3.5 shows the civilian occupations recommended by My Next Move for Veterans

---

[1] Its website can be found at https://www.mynextmove.org/vets/.

Table 3.5
Civilian Occupations Recommended by My Next Move for Veterans for Infantrymen (MOS 11B)

Civilian Occupation	Number of U.S. Jobs	Median Wages	Education at Entry	Distance Metric
Construction laborers (E1)	852,870	$31,090	High school diploma	64
Correctional officers and jailers (E4)	434,420	$39,780	High school diploma	76
Light truck or delivery services drivers (E4)	797,010	$29,570	High school diploma	49
Maintenance workers, machinery (E4)	90,730	$42,640	High school diploma	64
Police patrol officers (E4)	638,810	$56,810	High school diploma	80
Probation officers and correctional treatment specialists (E4)	86,810	$49,060	Bachelor's degree	55
Security guards (E4)	1,077,520	$24,410	High school diploma	42
First-line supervisors of transportation and material-moving machine and vehicle operators (E5)	197,000	$54,930	High school diploma	79
First-line supervisors of correctional officers (E5)	45,150	$57,970	High school diploma	71
Training and development specialists (E6)	239,500	$57,340	Bachelor's degree	53
Training and development managers (E7)	29,870	$101,930	Bachelor's degree	56
Emergency management directors (E7)	9,770	$64,360	Bachelor's degree	73

for infantrymen (11B), which are tailored to the pay grade of the transitioning soldier.

Note that only *one* of the occupations listed in Table 3.5, police patrol officers, would be considered a high-quality match based on a score of 80 or higher on our distance metric. My Next Move for Veterans also omits several other occupations that would be good matches for infantrymen, including firefighters; captains, mates, and pilots of water vessels; and structural iron and steel workers. Some occupations recommended by My Next Move for Veterans, such as construction laborers, delivery truck drivers, and security guards, appear to be particularly bad fits for infantrymen, based on both the distance metric and low median wages.

To examine in greater detail why these three occupations appear to be bad fits for infantrymen, we compared their average survey scores with those of infantrymen. First, we found that the average level and importance of KSAs and work attributes were lower across the board for construction laborers, delivery truck drivers, and security guards than for infantrymen. This is consistent with the relatively low wages paid in these occupations. Next, we identified the occupation attributes with the greatest gaps, in the sense that they were rated highly by infantrymen but were not considered important by the other three occupations. Those attributes are listed in Table 3.6. Many of the greatest gaps are in soft skills (shown in shaded cells), including leadership, teamwork, and training, managing, and supervising others. Note that while we defined only 25 percent of the O*NET attributes as directly associated with soft skills, more than half of the attributes listed in Table 3.6 are associated with soft skills.

Occupation Analysis for Combat Engineer (MOS 12B)

Based on Army's description of MOS 12B (Department of the Army, 2008a), the primary tasks of a combat engineer are to supervise or to serve as a member of an Army organization that is engaged in providing mobility, counter-mobility and survivability support to combat forces. Soldiers in this MOS perform basic demolition, mine warfare, and combat construction tasks. The occupation survey data give us additional insight into the job attributes of combat engineers that allow us to identify the closest-matching civilian occupations based on our distance metric.

Table 3.6
Occupation Attributes with the Greatest Gaps Between Infantrymen and Construction Laborers, Delivery Truck Drivers, and Security Guards

Knowledge	Skills	Abilities
Geography	Equipment maintenance	Night vision
Education and training	Instructing	Peripheral vision
Therapy and counseling	Equipment selection	Sound localization
		Explosive strength
		Dynamic strength
Work Activities (41 Questions)	**Work Context (57 Questions)**	**Work Styles (16 Questions)**
Guiding, directing and motivating subordinates	Public speaking	Adaptability/flexibility
Coaching and developing others	Responsibility for work outcomes and results	Social orientation
Training and teaching others	Exposed to whole body vibration	Leadership

NOTE: Soft skills are shown in shaded cells.

Top-Rated KSAs for Combat Engineers

First, we examine the top-rated KSAs and work attributes for combat engineers, shown in Table 3.7. As was the case with infantrymen, relatively few of the combat engineers' top-rated KSAs are associated with soft skills, with the exceptions of education and training and complex problem solving. Work attributes associated with soft skills include project planning, communication, and teamwork, as well as four of the five top-rated work styles.

Best-Matching Civilian Occupations for Combat Engineers

Due to their different mix of KSAs and work attributes, combat engineers have a larger number of high-quality civilian occupation matches than infantrymen. We found 92 high-quality matches that scored 80 or higher on our distance metric, 78 of which required less than a bachelor's degree at entry. Sixty of these high-quality matches were general civilian occupation matches that were common with four or more

Table 3.7
Top-Rated Occupation Attributes for Combat Engineers (MOS 12B)

Knowledge	Skills	Abilities
Engineering and technology (16.6)	Equipment maintenance (19.6)	Explosive strength (24.0)
Geography (15.6)	Mathematics (19.3)	Static strength (21.0)
Education and training (15.5)	Active listening (18.6)	Trunk strength (19.6)
Mathematics (15.5)	Coordination (18.5)	Night vision (21.5)
Public safety and security (15.3)	Complex problem solving (18.4)	Far vision (20.7)
		Depth perception (18.4)
		Stamina (20.3)
		Sound localization (18.3)
		Reaction time (18.3)
Work Activities	**Work Context**	**Work Styles**
Performing general physical activities (22.1)	Face-to-face discussions (4.7)	Attention to detail (4.7)
Identifying objects, actions, and events (22.1)	Contact with others (4.5)	Leadership (4.5)
Monitor processes, materials, or surroundings (21.9)	Work with work group or team (4.5)	Adaptability/flexibility (4.5)
Handling and moving objects (21.7)	Time pressure (4.5)	Stress tolerance (4.4)
Organizing, planning, and prioritizing work (21.2)	Outdoors, exposed to weather (4.4)	Self-control (4.4)

NOTES: For KSAs and work activities, score in parentheses is the product of the average importance score (scale of 1 to 5) and average level score (scale of 1 to 7); for work context and work styles, score in parentheses is on a scale of 1 to 5. Soft skills are shown in shaded cells.

MOSs, while 18 were MOS-specific matches. Tables 3.8 and 3.9 show the top ten general and MOS-specific matches, respectively, that meet our education criterion. They are also selected based on their combined rankings on the distance metric, job density in the U.S. economy, and median wages. Using these additional criteria, three of the most promising MOS-specific occupations that soldiers who served as combat engineers may want to pursue are carpenters, electrical power-line installers and repairers, and elevator installers and repairers.

Table 3.8
Top Ten General Occupational Matches for Combat Engineers (MOS 12B)

Civilian Occupation	Number of U.S. Jobs	Median Wages	Education at Entry	Distance Metric
Firefighters	308,790	$45,970	High school diploma	100
Captains, mates, and pilots of water vessels	30,690	$72,340	Postsecondary certification	95
First-line supervisors of mechanics, installers, and repairers	434,810	$62,150	High school diploma	95
First-line supervisors of fire fighting and prevention workers	59,870	$70,670	High school diploma	94
Aircraft mechanics and service technicians	116,830	$56,990	Postsecondary certification	90
First-line supervisors of construction trades and extraction workers	496,370	$60,990	High school diploma	90
Plumbers, pipefitters, and steamfitters	372,570	$50,660	Postsecondary certification	88
Electricians	566,930	$51,110	Postsecondary certification	87
Telecommunications equipment installers and repairers, except line installers	213,620	$55,190	Postsecondary certification	87
First-line supervisors of production and operating workers	592,830	$55,520	High school diploma	87

NOTE: Matches do not account for statistically similar occupational matches resulting from estimation variance.

We selected carpenters for a more detailed occupational comparison with combat engineers. It does not seem obvious that a carpenter would be a good match for a combat engineer, but it is one of the more promising MOS-specific occupation matches because of its relatively high prevalence in the U.S. economy. Table 3.10 shows the top-rated job attributes of carpenters and compares them with those of combat engineers. The numbers in parentheses indicate combat engineers' rankings of the same attributes, with soft skills shown in shaded cells. The strongest overlap is in work activities, where three of carpenters' top five attributes were also ranked in the top five by combat engineers. Several additional KSAs and work styles ranked highly by

Table 3.9
Top Ten MOS-Specific Occupational Matches for Combat Engineers (MOS 12B)

Civilian Occupation	Number of U.S. Jobs	Median Wages	Education at Entry	Distance Metric
Commercial divers	3,620	$45,890	Postsecondary certification	87
Electro-mechanical technicians	14,430	$53,070	Associate's degree	85
Elevator installers and repairers	20,590	$78,620	High school diploma	84
Carpenters	617,060	$40,820	High school diploma	84
Radio, cellular, and tower equipment installers and repairers	13,310	$47,950	Associate's degree	84
Drywall and ceiling tile installers	85,020	$38,100	High school diploma	83
Electrical power-line installers and repairers	114,540	$65,930	Postsecondary certification	83
Chefs and head cooks	118,130	$41,610	Associate's degree	82
Mobile heavy equipment mechanics, except engines	119,280	$47,580	Postsecondary certification	82
Tool and die makers	75,950	$48,890	Postsecondary certification	81

NOTE: Matches do not account for statistically similar occupational matches resulting from estimation variance.

Table 3.10
Top-Rated Occupation Attributes for Carpenters and Combat Engineers' (MOS 12B) Ratings of Those Attributes

Knowledge (33 Questions)	Skills (35 Questions)	Abilities (52 Questions)
Building and construction (10)	Coordination (4)	Trunk strength (6)
Mathematics (4)	Critical thinking (12)	Static strength (3)
Mechanical (9)	Monitoring (8)	Visualization (17)
Design (15)	Mathematics (2)	Manual dexterity (38)
Production and processing (26)	Time management (7)	Near vision (21)
		Extent flexibility (32)
		Multi-limb coordination (46)
		Oral comprehension (12)
Work Activities (41 Questions)	**Work Context (57 Questions)**	**Work Styles (16 Questions)**
Handling and moving objects (4)	Face-to-face discussions (1)	Attention to detail (1)
Performing general physical activities (1)	Wear common protective or safety equipment (8)	Dependability (7)
Organizing, planning and prioritizing work (5)	Work with work group or team (3)	Integrity (8)
Coordinating the work and activities of others (22)	Spend time standing (11)	Cooperation (9)
Communicating with supervisors, peers or subordinates (14)	Telephone (13)	Self-control (5)
	Frequency of decisionmaking (34)	
	Exposed to hazardous equipment (40)	
	Coordinate or lead others in work activities (9)	

NOTES: Attributes are listed in the order they are ranked by carpenters. Rankings by combat engineers are shown in parentheses. Soft skills are shown in shaded cells.

carpenters were also ranked in the top ten by combat engineers. The largest discrepancies in job attributes are production and processing knowledge, manual dexterity, extent flexibility[2] and multi-limb coordination (under abilities), and frequency of decisionmaking and exposure to hazardous equipment (under work context).

Comparison of Survey Matches for Combat Engineers with My Next Move for Veterans

My Next Move for Veterans provides only three recommended civilian occupations for combat engineers: construction laborers; explosives workers, ordnance handling experts, and blasters; and administrative services managers, for soldiers separating at pay grades E3, E5, and E6, respectively (see Table 3.11). Although explosives worker is a high-quality general match for combat engineer, it did not rank very highly on our additional criteria of job density and median wages. The other two occupations are not high-quality matches based on our distance metric. In addition, administrative services manager typically requires a bachelor's degree at entry, so some separating soldiers might not be considered qualified for this position. In contrast, our distance metric found 78 occupations that are high-quality matches for combat engineers and do not require a bachelor's degree (or higher) at entry.

Table 3.11
Civilian Occupations Recommended by My Next Move for Veterans for Combat Engineers (MOS 12B)

Civilian Occupation	Number of U.S. Jobs	Median Wages	Education at Entry	Distance Metric
Construction laborers (E3)	852,870	$31,090	High school diploma	73
Explosives workers, ordnance handling experts, and blasters (E5)	7,970	$52,140	High school diploma	90
Administrative services managers (E6)	268,730	$83,790	Bachelor's degree	61

[2] Extent flexibility is defined as the ability to bend, stretch, twist, or reach with your body, arms, and legs.

Occupational Analysis for Cannon Crewmember (MOS 13B)

Based on the Army's description of MOS 13B (Department of the Army, 2008a), the primary task of a cannon crewmember is to supervise or serve as a member of a field artillery cannon or ammunition section in support of long-range target engagement by indirect fire. Cannon crewmembers set fuses and charges on a variety of munitions, and use computer-generated fire direction data to set elevation of the cannon tube for loading and firing. Crewmembers are also responsible for transporting and managing both cannon and artillery ammunition. The O*NET surveys reveal additional information about the KSAs and work attributes of cannon crewmembers that can be compared with those of civilian occupations.

Top-Rated KSAs for Cannon Crewmembers

Table 3.12 shows the top-rated KSAs and work attributes for cannon crewmembers, with soft skills shown in shaded cells. Note that cannon crewmembers rated cognitive abilities, such as selective attention (the ability to concentrate on a task without being distracted), time sharing (the ability to shift back and forth between two or more activities or sources of information), and oral expression, more highly than infantrymen and combat engineers, who gave higher ratings to psychomotor and sensory abilities. All of the cannon crewmembers' top-rated work activities and work styles are associated with soft skills such as communication, leadership, and training, managing, and supervising others.

Best-Matching Civilian Occupations for Cannon Crewmember

We found a total of 48 high-quality civilian occupation matches for cannon crewmembers that scored 80 or higher on our distance metric, none of which required a bachelor's or higher degree at entry. Forty-one of these occupations were general matches that were shared by four or more of the MOSs we analyzed, and seven were MOS-specific matches. Table 3.13 lists the top ten general matches, selected based on their combined rankings on the distance metric, job density in the U.S. economy, and median wages. Table 3.14 lists all of the MOS-specific matches.

Table 3.12
Top-Rated Occupation Attributes for Cannon Crewmembers (MOS 13B)

Knowledge	Skills	Abilities
Education and training (15.8)	Equipment maintenance (27.2)	Selective attention (21.6)
Administration and management (13.1)	Troubleshooting (21.8)	Oral expression (21.6)
Mechanical (12.7)	Active listening (21.3)	Time sharing (20.6)
Geography (11.4)	Instructing (21.2)	Night vision (20.6)
Mathematics (11.0)	Management of personnel resources (20.6)	Reaction time (20.4)
Work Activities	**Work Context**	**Work Styles**
Training and teaching others (21.9)	Face-to-face discussions (5)	Achievement/effort (4.6)
Coaching and developing others (21.8)	Outdoors, exposed to weather (5)	Attention to detail (4.6)
Guiding, directing, and motivating subordinates (20.7)	Contact with others (4.9)	Stress tolerance (4.5)
Communicating with supervisors, peers, or subordinates (20.6)	Work with work group or team (4.8)	Dependability (4.5)
Establishing and maintaining interpersonal relationships (19.6)	Sounds, noise levels are distracting or uncomfortable (4.8)	Persistence (4.4)

NOTES: For KSAs and work activities, score in parentheses is the product of the average importance score (scale of 1 to 5) and average level score (scale of 1 to 7); for work context and work styles, score in parentheses is on a scale of 1 to 5. Soft skills are shown in shaded cells.

We selected extraction worker's helper for a more detailed comparison with the KSAs of cannon crewmembers. The primary tasks of an extraction worker's helper are to help extraction craft workers, such as earth drillers, blasters and explosives workers, derrick operators, and mining machine operators, by performing duties of lesser skill. These duties include supplying and maintaining equipment and cleaning the work area. This position would be an entry-level position after a single

Table 3.13
Top Ten General Occupational Matches for Cannon Crewmembers (MOS 13B)

Civilian Occupation	Number of U.S. Jobs	Median Wages	Education at Entry	Distance Metric
Captains, mates, and pilots of water vessels	30,690	$72,340	Postsecondary certification	94
Firefighters	308,790	$45,970	High school diploma	92
Service unit operators, oil, gas, and mining	62,080	$44,970	High school diploma	90
Rotary drill operators, oil and gas	26,480	$53,160	Less than high school	89
First-line supervisors of fire fighting and prevention workers	59,870	$70,670	High school diploma	88
First-line supervisors of mechanics, installers, and repairers	434,810	$62,150	High school diploma	87
Chemical plant and system operators	37,490	$55,900	High school diploma	87
First-line supervisors of production and operating workers	592,830	$55,520	High school diploma	84
Petroleum pump system operators, refinery operators, and gaugers	41,700	$62,830	High school diploma	84
Aircraft mechanics and service technicians	116,830	$56,990	Postsecondary certification	83

NOTE: Matches do not account for statistically similar occupational matches resulting from estimation variance.

enlistment period was served and would likely lead to opportunities to become an extraction craft worker with higher median wages.

In Table 3.15, we show the KSAs and work attributes that extraction worker's helpers indicate are most important to their jobs. The strongest overlap appears to be in work context, with three of extraction worker's helpers' top-rated attributes also rated in the top five by

Table 3.14
MOS-Specific Occupational Matches for Cannon Crewmembers (MOS 13B)

Civilian Occupation	Number of U.S. Jobs	Median Wages	Education at Entry	Distance Metric
Electrical power-line installers and repairers	114,540	65,930	Postsecondary certification	86
Rail-track laying and maintenance equipment operators	14,820	51,840	High school diploma	83
Solar photovoltaic installers	5,170	40,020	High school diploma	82
Helpers—roofers	11,640	26,060	High school diploma	82
Helpers—extraction workers	24,130	34,480	High school diploma	81
Segmental pavers	1,130	32,180	High school diploma	81
Reinforcing iron and rebar workers	18,530	50,020	High school diploma	80

NOTE: Matches do not account for statistically similar occupational matches resulting from estimation variance.

cannon crewmembers. Most of the other categories have at least one attribute rated in the top five by cannon crewmembers, with additional attributes rated in the top ten. However, there are also some potential gaps in knowledge attributes such as engineering and technology and production and processing; abilities such as multi-limb coordination, control precision, and visualization; work activities such as handling and moving objects and inspecting equipment, structures, or material; and work context such as using hands to handle or control objects or tools and freedom to make decisions.

Comparison of Survey Matches for Cannon Crewmembers with My Next Move for Veterans

My Next Move for Veterans recommends 13 civilian occupations for cannon crewmembers, ranging from pay grade E2 through E6, shown in Table 3.16. Only one of these matches, hazardous materials removal

Table 3.15
Top-Rated Occupation Attributes for Extraction Worker's Helpers and Cannon Crewmembers' (MOS 13B) Ratings of Those Attributes

Knowledge (33 Questions)	Skills (35 Questions)	Abilities (52 Questions)
Mechanical (3)	Operation monitoring (9)	Multi-limb coordination (45)
Public safety and security (8)	Repairing (8)	Reaction time (5)
Law and government (16)	Equipment maintenance (1)	Static strength (23)
Engineering and technology (21)	Monitoring (12)	Trunk strength (16)
Production and processing (25)	Operation and control (7)	Control precision (39)
		Far vision (11)
		Depth perception (18)
		Visualization (35)
Work Activities (41 Questions)	**Work Context (57 Questions)**	**Work Styles (16 Questions)**
Operating vehicles, mechanized devices, or equipment (16)	Wear common protective or safety equipment (10)	Dependability (4)
Handling and moving objects (25)	Spend time using your hands to handle, control, or feel objects, tools, or controls (36)	Independence (15)
Monitor processes, materials, or surroundings (20)	Exposed to hazardous equipment (27)	Adaptability/flexibility (7)
Inspecting equipment, structures, or material (35)	Face-to-face discussions (1)	Integrity (11)
Repairing and maintaining mechanical equipment (6)	Sounds, noise levels are distracting or uncomfortable (5)	Initiative (6)
	Spend time standing (12)	
	Work with work group or team (4)	
	Freedom to make decisions (39)	

NOTES: Attributes are listed in the order they are ranked by extraction worker's helpers. Rankings by cannon crewmembers are shown in parentheses. Soft skills are shown in shaded cells.

Table 3.16
Civilian Occupations Recommended by My Next Move for Veterans for Cannon Crewmembers (MOS 13B)

Civilian Occupation	Number of U.S. Jobs	Median Wages	Education at Entry	Distance Metric
Radio operators (E2)	1,100	$46,380	High school diploma	58
Construction laborers (E3)	852,870	$31,090	High school diploma	73
Correctional officers and jailers (E4)	434,420	$39,780	High school diploma	72
Bus drivers, transit and intercity (E4)	158,050	$37,470	High school diploma	72
Light truck or delivery services drivers (E4)	797,010	$29,570	High school diploma	59
Hazardous materials removal workers (E5)	42,250	$38,520	High school diploma	87
Emergency medical technicians and paramedics (E5)	235,760	$31,700	Postsecondary certification	73
Electro-mechanical technicians (E5)	14,430	$53,070	Associate's degree	76
Equal opportunity representatives and officers (E6)*				
Vocational education teachers, postsecondary (E6)	121,200	$48,360	Postsecondary certification	62
General and operations managers (E6)	2,049,870	$97,270	Associate's degree	66
First-line supervisors of transportation and material-moving machine and vehicle operators (E6)	197,000	$54,930	High school diploma	79
Emergency management directors (E6)	9,770	$64,360	Bachelor's degree	68

* Not listed in Standard Occupation Classification system. Matches do not account for statistically similar occupational matches resulting from estimation variance.

workers, would be considered a high-quality match based on our distance metric. It is a general match common to at least four MOSs we analyzed, but did not rank as high as other occupations listed in Table 3.13 because of relatively low job density and median wages. Other than hazardous materials removal workers, none of the other occupations recommended by My Next Move for Veterans has a distance metric above 79. Most of the other occupations have distance metrics in the low 70s, with some scores as low as 58 or 59 for radio operators and light truck or delivery services drivers.

Occupational Analysis of Calvary Scout (MOS 19D)

According to the Army's description of MOS 19D (Department of the Army, 2008a), a cavalry scout is responsible for assessing terrain conditions, understanding the geography, and reporting enemy position, strength, and armaments to the commander during battle. Cavalry scouts engage the enemy in the field, track and report enemy activity, and direct the employment of weapon systems to their locations. The Army requires these soldiers to perform the following duties: secure and prepare ammunition on scout vehicles; perform navigation during combat; report information on terrain, weather, and the enemy; and collect data to classify routes, tunnels, and bridges. The O*NET surveys reveal additional information about the KSAs and work attributes of cavalry scouts that we can compare with civilian occupations.

Top-Rated KSAs for Cavalry Scouts

Table 3.17 shows the top-rated occupation attributes for cavalry scouts, based on our survey sample. Highly rated soft skills include critical thinking, decisionmaking, communication, leadership, and project planning. Similar to most of the other maneuver, fires, and effects MOSs we analyzed, the abilities rated the highest by cavalry scouts are classified by O*NET as sensory and psychomotor abilities.

Table 3.17
Top-Rated Occupation Attributes for Cavalry Scouts (MOS 19D)

Knowledge	Skills	Abilities
Geography (20.8)	Coordination (19.3)	Night vision (25.9)
		Peripheral vision (25.5)
		Far vision (25.1)
		Depth perception (24.5)
Public safety and security (15.6)	Equipment maintenance (18.8)	Trunk strength (22.8)
		Static strength (22.5)
Education and training (13.3)	Active listening (18.1)	Reaction time (22.4)
Administration and management (12.1)	Critical thinking (16.4)	Sound localization (22.4) Auditory attention (21.5)
Mechanical (11.3)	Judgement and decisionmaking (16.1)	Stamina (22.1)

Work Activities	Work Context	Work Styles
Performing general physical activities (22.8)	Face-to-face discussions (4.8)	Leadership (4.6)
Handling and moving objects (20.3)	Contact with others (4.8)	Stress tolerance (4.6)
Guiding, directing, and motivating subordinates (16.3)	Work with work group or team (4.6)	Attention to detail (4.6)
Communicating with supervisors, peers, or subordinates (15.4)	Outdoors, exposed to weather (4.6)	Adaptability/flexibility (4.5)
Organizing, planning, and prioritlzing work (15.1)	Time pressure (4.4)	Dependability (4.5)

NOTES: For KSAs and work activities, score in parentheses is the product of the average importance score (scale of 1 to 5) and average level score (scale of 1 to 7); for work context and work styles, score in parentheses is on a scale of 1 to 5. Soft skills are shown in shaded cells.

Best-Matching Civilian Occupations for Cavalry Scouts

We found a total of 70 high-quality matching civilian occupations for cavalry scouts that scored 80 or higher on our distance metric, of which 68 require less than a bachelor's degree at entry. Fifty-five of the occupations are general matches shared by four or more MOSs we analyzed. The remaining 13 occupations are MOS-specific matches. The top ten general and MOS-specific matches, selected based on their combined rankings on our distance metric, job density in the U.S. economy, and median wages, are shown in Tables 3.18 and 3.19, respectively.

Among the 13 MOS-specific matches that we found, we selected railroad conductors and yardmasters for a more detailed comparison with cavalry scouts because they score well on our distance metric, receive annual median pay of about $55,000, and do not require additional training, education, or certification prior to employment. Railroad conductors and yardmasters coordinate the activities of engine crews within a railroad yard, industrial plant, or similar location. Conductors coordinate the activities of train crews on passenger or freight trains. Yardmasters review train schedules and switching orders and coordinate activities of workers engaged in railroad traffic operations, such as the makeup or breakup of trains and yard switching (see Bureau of Labor Statistics, 2010).

Table 3.20 shows the top-rated occupation attributes of railroad conductors and yardmasters and how they are rated by cavalry scouts. The strongest overlap is in work context, where four attributes are rated in the top five by cavalry scouts. Most other categories include two attributes rated in the top five by cavalry scouts. The exception is abilities, where only far vision is rated in the top five by cavalry scouts. Most of the largest potential gaps are also in abilities, primarily cognitive abilities, such as oral expression, problem sensitivity, information ordering, and deductive reasoning.

Comparison of Survey Matches for Cavalry Scouts with My Next Move for Veterans

Table 3.21 shows the occupations recommended by My Next Move for Veterans for cavalry scouts. Only one of these occupations, hazardous materials removal workers, would be considered a high-quality match

Table 3.18
Top Ten General Occupational Matches for Cavalry Scouts (MOS 19D)

Civilian Occupation	Number of U.S. Jobs	Median Wages	Education at Entry	Distance Metric
Captains, mates, and pilots of water vessels	30,690	$72,340	Postsecondary certification	96
Firefighters	308,790	$45,970	High school diploma	96
Chemical plant and system operators	37,490	$55,900	High school diploma	88
First-line supervisors of fire fighting and prevention workers	59,870	$70,670	High school diploma	88
First-line supervisors of mechanics, installers, and repairers	434,810	$62,150	High school diploma	87
First-line supervisors of production and operating workers	592,830	$55,520	High school diploma	86
Plumbers, pipefitters, and steamfitters	372,570	$50,660	Postsecondary certification	86
Electricians	566,930	$51,110	Postsecondary certification	84
First-line supervisors of construction trades and extraction workers	496,370	$60,990	High school diploma	82
Police and sheriff's patrol officers	638,810	$56,810	High school diploma	82

NOTE: Matches do not account for statistically similar occupational matches resulting from estimation variance.

based on our distance metric. It is not listed in Table 3.18 because it did not rank as well on job density or median wages as other general matches. Particularly poor matches for cavalry scouts are security guards (with a distance metric of 53) and first-line supervisors of office and administrative support workers (with a distance metric of 54). While both of these jobs are quite common, with more than 1 million workers in each occupation, they are relatively low-paying and are

Table 3.19
Top Ten MOS-Specific Occupational Matches for Cavalry Scouts (MOS 19D)

Civilian Occupation	Number of U.S. Jobs	Median Wages	Education at Entry	Distance Metric
Railroad conductors and yardmasters	42,900	$54,770	High school diploma	84
Carpenters	617,060	$40,820	High school diploma	83
Rail-track laying and maintenance equipment operators	14,820	$51,840	High school diploma	83
Mobile heavy equipment mechanics, except engines	119,280	$47,580	Postsecondary certification	82
Railroad brake, signal, and switch operators	21,060	$52,360	High school diploma	82
Subway and streetcar operators	11,300	$62,130	High school diploma	82
Extruding and drawing machine setters, operators, and tenders, metal and plastic	72,520	$32,610	High school diploma	81
Transit and railroad police	3,380	$51,690	Associate's degree	81
Carpet installers	26,050	$35,880	High school diploma	81
Reinforcing iron and rebar workers	18,530	$50,020	High school diploma	80

NOTE: Matches do not account for statistically similar occupational matches resulting from estimation variance.

unlikely to take advantage of the skills developed by cavalry scouts in the Army. Some of the other occupations recommended by My Next Move for Veterans require a bachelor's degree at entry.

Table 3.20
Top-Rated Occupation Attributes for Railroad Conductors and Yardmasters and Cavalry Scouts' (MOS 19D) Ratings of Those Attributes

Knowledge (33 Questions)	Skills (35 Questions)	Abilities (52 Questions)
Transportation (7)	Monitoring (7)	Oral expression (32)
Public safety and security (2)	Coordination (1)	Oral comprehension (22)
Education and training (3)	Critical thinking (4)	Problem sensitivity (31)
English language (6)	Time management (6)	Far vision (3)
Customer and personal service (23)	Speaking (14)	Information ordering (44)
		Deductive reasoning (34)
		Speech clarity (29)
		Near vision (14)
Work Activities (41 Questions)	**Work Context (57 Questions)**	**Work Styles (16 Questions)**
Handling and moving objects (2)	Face-to-face discussions (1)	Dependability (5)
Performing general physical activities (1)	Wear common protective or safety equipment (7)	Integrity (7)
Getting information (14)	Outdoors, exposed to weather (4)	Attention to detail (3)
Inspecting equipment, structures, or material (19)	Sounds, noise levels are distracting or uncomfortable (11)	Self-control (6)
Identifying objects, actions, and events (7)	Contact with others (2)	Independence (13)
	Work with work group or team (3)	
	In an enclosed vehicle or equipment (12)	
	Exposed to contaminants (22)	

NOTES: Attributes are listed in the order they are ranked by railroad conductors and yardmasters. Rankings by cavalry scouts are shown in parentheses. Soft skills are shown in shaded cells.

Table 3.21
Civilian Occupations Recommended by My Next Move for Veterans for Cavalry Scouts (MOS 19D)

Civilian Occupation	Number of U.S. Jobs	Median Wages	Education at Entry	Distance Metric
Radio operators (E2)	1,100	$46,380	High school diploma	62
Security guards (E2)	1,077,520	$24,410	High school diploma	53
Construction laborers (E2)	852,870	$31,090	High school diploma	74
Correctional officers and jailers (E4)	434,420	$39,780	High school diploma	78
Stock clerks—stockroom, warehouse, or storage yard (E4)	1,878,860	$22,850	High school diploma	56
Maintenance workers, machinery (E4)	90,730	$42,640	High school diploma	75
First-line supervisors of correctional officers (E5)	45,150	$57,970	High school diploma	74
Hazardous materials removal workers (E5)	42,250	$38,520	High school diploma	82
Training and development specialists (E6)	239,500	$57,340	Bachelor's degree	54
First-line supervisors of office and administrative support workers (E6)	1,404,070	$50,780	High school diploma	54
Transportation managers (E7)*	106,000	$85,400	Bachelor's degree	64
Storage and distribution managers (E7)*	106,000	$85,400	Bachelor's degree	64
Administrative services managers (E7)	268,730	$83,790	Bachelor's degree	56

*The Bureau of Labor Statistics lists Transportation, Storage, and Distribution Managers as a single occupation.

Occupational Analysis for M1 Armor Crewman (MOS 19K)

Based on the Army's description of MOS 19K (Department of the Army, 2008a), an M1 armor crewman is responsible for operating armored equipment such as the M1A2 Abrams tank to destroy enemy positions. The job duties require operating tracked and wheeled vehicles over various terrains, using communications equipment, loading and firing guns, and reading maps, compasses and battle plans. We use the O*NET survey data to identify the KSAs and work attributes of M1 armor crewmen for comparison with civilian occupations.

Top-Rated KSAs for Armor Crewmen

Table 3.22 shows the top-rated occupation attributes for M1 armor crewmen. None of the top-rated KSAs are associated with soft skills, but several work attributes are associated leadership, communication, and teamwork.

Best-Matching Civilian Occupations for M1 Armor Crewmen

Based on our distance metric, we identified 13 high-quality occupation matches for M1 armor crewmen, none of which require a bachelor's degree or higher at entry (see Table 3.23). All of these occupations are general matches that are shared by four or more MOSs.

Since we have already discussed the match between firefighters and infantrymen, here we consider the occupational attributes that are shared by captains, mates, and pilots of water vessels and M1 armor crewmen. Table 3.24 shows the top-rated attributes of captains, mates, and pilots of water vessels and how they are ranked by M1 armor crewman. The strongest overlap is in work styles, where four of top five attributes selected by captains, mates, and pilots of water vessels are also in the top five for M1 armor crewmen. Two knowledge and work context attributes are also in the top five for M1 armor crewmen. The largest potential gaps are in control precision (the ability to quickly and repeatedly adjust the controls of a machine or vehicle to exact positions), structured versus unstructured work, and freedom to make decisions.

Table 3.22
Top-Rated Occupation Attributes for M1 Armor Crewmen (MOS 19K)

Knowledge	Skills	Abilities
Mechanical (21.5)	Equipment maintenance (26.8)	Night vision (27.0)
Public safety and security (16.6)	Repairing (22.6)	Peripheral vision (25.2)
English language (14.2)	Active listening (22.0)	Depth perception (25.0)
Geography (14.0)	Management of personnel resources (21.6)	Far vision (21.4)
Administration and management (13.5)	Time management (21.3)	Static strength (25.5)
		Explosive strength (22.7)
		Trunk strength (21.7)
		Reaction time (23.1)
		Sound localization (22.4)
		Speed of limb movement (22.2)
Work Activities	**Work Context**	**Work Styles**
Performing general physical activities (26.1)	Contact with others (4.9)	Attention to detail (5)
Handling and moving objects (24.9)	Face-to-face discussions (4.8)	Leadership (4.9)
Operating vehicles, mechanized devices, or equipment (24.1)	Work with work group or team (4.6)	Adaptability/flexibility (4.8)
Guiding, directing, and motivating subordinates (24.1)	Outdoors, exposed to weather (4.5)	Dependability (4.8)
Repairing and maintaining mechanical equipment (24.0)	Physical proximity (4.4)	Integrity (4.8)

NOTES: For KSAs and work activities, score in parentheses is the product of the average importance score (scale of 1 to 5) and average level score (scale of 1 to 7); for work context and work styles, score in parentheses is on a scale of 1 to 5. Soft skills are shown in shaded cells.

Table 3.23
Occupational Matches for M1 Armor Crewmen (MOS 19K)

Civilian Occupation	Number of U.S. Jobs	Median Wages	Education at Entry	Distance Metric
Firefighters	308,790	$45,970	High school diploma	92
Captains, mates, and pilots of water vessels	30,690	$72,340	Postsecondary certification	88
First-line supervisors of mechanics, installers, and repairers	434,810	$62,150	High school diploma	87
Millwrights	39,290	$50,460	High school diploma	86
Ship engineers	10,060	$68,100	Postsecondary certification	85
First-line supervisors of fire fighting and prevention workers	59,870	$70,670	High school diploma	84
Heating, air conditioning, and refrigeration mechanics and installers	261,390	$44,630	Postsecondary certification	83
Septic tank servicers and sewer pipe cleaners	24,350	$34,810	Less than high school	82
Aircraft mechanics and service technicians	116,830	$56,990	Postsecondary certification	82
Manufactured building and mobile home installers	3,280	$29,600	Less than high school	81
Fire inspectors and investigators	11,370	$56,130	Some college	80
Automotive service technicians and mechanics	633,390	$37,120	Postsecondary certification	80
Service unit operators, oil, gas, and mining	62,080	$44,970	High school diploma	80

NOTE: Matches do not account for statistically similar occupational matches resulting from estimation variance.

Table 3.24
Top-Rated Occupation Attributes for Captains, Mates, and Pilots of Water Vessels and M1 Armor Crewmen's (MOS 19K) Ratings of Those Attributes

Knowledge (33 Questions)	Skills (35 Questions)	Abilities (52 Questions)
Public safety and security (2)	Operation and control (13)	Far vision (10)
Transportation (7)	Coordination (9)	Problem sensitivity (13)
Customer and personal service (19)	Critical thinking (17)	Oral comprehension (14)
Education and training (6)	Speaking (20)	Oral expression (22)
Administration and management (5)	Judgment and decisionmaking (7)	Spatial orientation (19)
		Control precision (36)
		Selective attention (12)
		Glare sensitivity (15)

Work Activities (41 Questions)	Work Context (57 Questions)	Work Styles (16 Questions)
Operating vehicles, mechanized devices, or equipment (3)	Face-to-face discussions (2)	Dependability (4)
Controlling machines and processes (7)	Impact of decisions on co-workers or company results (20)	Leadership (2)
Making decisions and solving problems (14)	Frequency of decisionmaking (13)	Integrity (5)
Inspecting equipment, structures, or material (12)	Telephone (31)	Stress tolerance (6)
Getting information (16)	Work with work group or team (3)	Attention to detail (1)
	Structured versus unstructured work (38)	
	Freedom to make decisions (33)	
	Sounds, noise levels are distracting or uncomfortable (7)	

NOTES: Attributes are listed in the order they are ranked by captains, mates, and pilots of water vessels. Rankings by M1 armor crewmen are shown in parentheses. Soft skills are shown in shaded cells.

Comparison of Survey Matches for M1 Armor Crewmen with My Next Move for Veterans

My Next Move for Veterans recommends the same group of 13 civilian occupations for M1 armor crewmen as it does for cavalry scouts (see Table 3.25). Across the board, these occupations score lower on our distance metric for M1 armor crewmen than they do for cavalry scouts, so even the highest-scoring occupation, hazardous materials removal workers, does not meet the threshold of 80 for a high-quality match. Other recommended matches, such as security guards and stock clerks, are very low-quality matches and also have median wages that are well below the U.S. annual median wage of about $47,000.

Occupational Matches for Military Police (MOS 31B)

According to the Army's description of MOS 31B, military police protect lives and property on Army installations by enforcing military laws and regulations. They also control traffic, prevent crime, and respond to all emergencies. The job duties of military police include law enforcement patrols; interviewing witnesses, victims, and suspects in investigations; crime scene security and processing; and arresting and charging soldiers suspected of criminal activity (Department of the Army, 2008a). We use the O*NET surveys to characterize the KSAs and work attributes of military police for comparison with civilian occupations.

Top-Rated KSAs for Military Police

Table 3.26 shows the top-rated occupation attributes for military police. Several of their top-rated skills and abilities are associated with soft skills, particularly oral and written communication. Their top-rated work attributes are associated with additional soft skills, such as leadership, management, and teamwork. In addition, the knowledge and work activities rated highly by military police emphasize working with the public more than other MOSs we have discussed so far in this chapter.

Table 3.25
Civilian Occupations Recommended by My Next Move for Veterans for M1 Armor Crewmen (MOS 19K)

Civilian Occupation	Number of U.S. Jobs	Median Wages	Education at Entry	Distance Metric
Radio operators (E2)	1,100	$46,380	High school diploma	53
Security guards (E2)	1,077,520	$24,410	High school diploma	36
Construction laborers (E2)	852,870	$31,090	High school diploma	61
Correctional officers and jailers (E4)	434,420	$39,780	High school diploma	69
Stock clerks—stockroom, warehouse, or storage yard (E4)	1,878,860	$22,850	High school diploma	38
Maintenance workers, machinery (E4)	90,730	$42,640	High school diploma	66
First-line supervisors of correctional officers (E5)	45,150	$57,970	High school diploma	70
Hazardous materials removal workers (E5)	42,250	$38,520	High school diploma	78
Training and development specialists (E6)	239,500	$57,340	Bachelor's degree	49
First-line supervisors of office and administrative support workers (E6)	1,404,070	$50,780	High school diploma	49
Transportation managers (E7)*	106,000	$85,400	Bachelor's degree	55
Storage and distribution managers (E7)*	106,000	$85,400	Bachelor's degree	55
Administrative services managers (E7)	268,730	$83,790	Bachelor's degree	49

*The Bureau of Labor Statistics lists Transportation, Storage, and Distribution Managers as a single occupation. Matches do not account for statistically similar occupational matches resulting from estimation variance.

Table 3.26
Top-Rated Occupation Attributes for Military Police (MOS 31B)

Knowledge	Skills	Abilities
Public safety and security (25.6)	Active listening (22.6)	Reaction time (23.5)
Customer and personal service (22.9)	Speaking (22.2)	Far vision (22.6)
	Critical thinking (20.5)	Near vision (20.7)
	Persuasion (17.7)	Peripheral vision (20.1)
Law and government (20.2)	Writing (17.6)	Oral comprehension (21.9)
English language (15.3)		Speech clarity (21.8)
Administration and management (13.6)		Written comprehension (20.5)
Work Activities	**Work Context**	**Work Styles**
Performing for or working directly with the public (25.3)	Face-to-face discussions (4.8)	Integrity (4.8)
Resolving conflicts and negotiating with others (24.5)	Contact with others (4.8)	Self-control (4.8)
Performing general physical activities (23.0)	Work with work group or team (4.6)	Attention to detail (4.8)
Assisting and caring for others (22.9)	Telephone (4.6)	Leadership (4.7)
Updating and using relevant knowledge (22.2)	Responsibility for outcomes and results (4.5)	Adaptability/flexibility (4.6)

NOTES: For KSAs and work activities, score in parentheses is the product of importance (scale of 1 to 5) and level (scale of 1 to 7); for work context and work styles, score in parentheses is on a scale of 1 to 5. Soft skills are shown in shaded cells.

Best-Matching Civilian Occupations for Military Police

Based on our distance metric, we found a total of 46 civilian occupations that rated 80 or higher for military police. Of these occupations, 33 require less than a bachelor's degree at entry. Thirty are general matches that are also shared by four or more MOSs that we analyzed. The remaining three are MOS-specific matches: gaming managers, transit and railroad police, and animal control officers. Each of these occupations is, however, quite rare in the U.S. economy. Part of the reason for these obscure matches for military police is that we have classified police and sheriff's patrol officers as a high-quality general match for several of the MOSs we analyzed, not just military police. Tables 3.27 and 3.28 show the top ten general matches, selected based on their combined rankings on the distance metric, job density in the U.S. economy, and median wages, and all the MOS-specific matches, respectively.

Because so many military-civilian occupation crosswalks recommend that soldiers investigate police occupations, we thought it would be worthwhile to compare military police with civilian police, both to point out the highlights of the match quality and to illustrate that the jobs are likely to have some differences between the military and civilian sectors. Table 3.29 shows the top-rated occupation attributes of civilian police or sheriff's officers and how they are ranked by military police. The amount of overlap is striking. In most categories, three or four of police and sheriff's patrol officers' top-rated attributes are also rated in the top five by military police. There are only a few potential gaps. In the skills category, civilian police indicate that social perceptiveness and reading comprehension are important, but they are not rated as highly by military police. Inductive and deductive reasoning play a strong role (fourth and fifth most important abilities) for civilian police officers but are not in the top 20 most important abilities for military police.

Table 3.27
Top Ten General Occupational Matches for Military Police (MOS 31B)

Civilian Occupation	Number of U.S. Jobs	Median Wages	Education at Entry	Distance Metric
First-line supervisors of police and detectives	101,420	$80,930	High school diploma	96
Firefighters	308,790	$45,970	High school diploma	94
First-line supervisors of fire fighting and prevention workers	59,870	$70,670	High school diploma	94
Police and sheriff's patrol officers	638,810	$56,810	High school diploma	93
Detectives and criminal investigators	108,720	$79,870	High school diploma	89
First-line supervisors of transportation and material-moving machine and vehicle operators	197,000	$54,930	High school diploma	88
Captains, mates, and pilots of water vessels	30,690	$72,340	Postsecondary certification	87
First-line supervisors of mechanics, installers, and repairers	434,810	$62,150	High school diploma	85
Registered nurses	2,687,310	$66,640	Associate's degree	84
First-line supervisors of construction trades and extraction workers	496,370	$60,990	High school diploma	81

NOTE: Matches do not account for statistically similar occupational matches resulting from estimation variance.

Table 3.28
MOS-Specific Occupational Matches for Military Police (MOS 31B)

Civilian Occupation	Number of U.S. Jobs	Median Wages	Education at Entry	Distance Metric
Transit and railroad police	3,380	$51,690	Associate's degree	84
Gaming managers	3,870	$67,310	High school diploma	82
Animal control workers	13,450	$32,560	High school diploma	81

NOTE: Matches do not account for statistically similar occupational matches resulting from estimation variance.

Comparison of Survey Matches for Military Police with My Next Move for Veterans

In Table 3.30, we show the occupations recommended for military police by My Next Move for Veterans, along with the score for our distance metric (in the far right column). My Next Move for Veterans lists 36 occupation matches for military police, many more than any of the other MOSs we have examined so far. The recommendations range from crossing guards for E3s to emergency management directors for E8s. We note that a crossing guard is a terrible match based on our distance metric, with a score of 34 out of 100. It seems clear that a former military policeman (or woman) is unlikely to be utilizing the skills he or she developed in the Army as a crossing guard. A similar story is seen for interviewers[3] and security guards. Conversely, there are a number of high-quality matches (80 points and higher). Overall, our distance metric indicates that some of these occupations make much better use than others of the KSAs that military police develop in the Army.

We also note that seven of the occupations recommended by My Next Move for Veterans are not listed in the SOC system, so we cannot evaluate them using our distance metric. An additional eight occupa-

[3] The job duties of an interviewer are described by the Bureau of Labor Statistics as follows: Interview persons by telephone, mail, in person, or by other means for the purpose of completing forms, applications, or questionnaires. Ask specific questions, record answers, and assist persons with completing form. May sort, classify, and file forms.

Table 3.29
Top-Rated Occupation Attributes for Police and Sheriff's Patrol Officers and Military Policemen's (MOS 31B) Ratings of Those Attributes

Knowledge (33 Questions)	Skills (35 Questions)	Abilities (52 Questions)
Public safety and security (1)	Active listening (1)	Problem sensitivity (14)
Law and government (3)	Critical thinking (3)	Oral expression (15)
Customer and personal service (2)	Speaking (2)	Oral comprehension (3)
Psychology (10)	Social perceptiveness (16)	Inductive reasoning (24)
English language (4)	Reading comprehension (15)	Deductive reasoning (26)
		Near vision (5)
		Reaction time (1)
		Written comprehension (6)

Work Activities (41 Questions)	Work Context (57 Questions)	Work Styles (16 Questions)
Identifying objects, actions, and events (10)	Telephone (4)	Integrity (1)
Resolving conflicts and negotiating with others (2)	Deal with external customers (16)	Self-control (2)
Performing for or working directly with the public (1)	Frequency of decisionmaking (19)	Dependability (11)
Monitor processes, materials, or surroundings (29)	Contact with others (2)	Stress tolerance (7)
Making decisions and solving problems (13)	Deal with unpleasant or angry people (12)	Attention to detail (3)
	Impact of decisions on co-workers or company results (18)	
	Work with work group or team (3)	
	Face-to-face discussions (1)	

NOTES: Attributes are listed in the order they are ranked by police and sheriff's patrol officers. Rankings by military police are shown in parentheses. Soft skills are shown in shaded cells.

Table 3.30
Civilian Occupations Recommended by My Next Move for Veterans for Military Police (MOS 31B)

Civilian Occupation	Number of U.S. Jobs	Median Wages	Education at Entry	Distance Metric
Crossing guards (E3)	66,310	$24,750	High school diploma	34
Animal control workers (E3)	13,450	$32,560	High school diploma	81
Parking enforcement workers (E3)	8,680	$36,570	High school diploma	59
Gaming surveillance officers and gaming investigators (3)	10,030	$29,840	High school diploma	77
Office clerks, general (E3)	2,889,970	$28,670	High school diploma	50
Interviewers, except eligibility and loan (E4)	190,710	$30,790	High school diploma	42
Police identification and records officers (E4)*				
Transportation security screeners (E4)	43,220	$38,090	High school diploma	71
Animal trainers (E4)	11,170	$25,770	High school diploma	69
Computer operators (E4)	58,060	$39,590	Associate's degree	64
Security guards (E4)	1,077,520	$24,410	High school diploma	47
Police patrol officers (E4)**	638,810	$56,810	High school diploma	93
Immigration and customs inspectors (E4)*				
Bailiffs (E4)	16,310	$38,150	High school diploma	61
Transit and railroad police (E4)	3,380	$51,690	Associate's degree	84
First-line supervisors of correctional officers (E5)	45,150	$57,970	High school diploma	82
First-line supervisors of police and detectives (E5)	101,420	$80,930	High school diploma	96
Eligibility interviewers, government programs (E5)	122,400	$42,200	High school diploma	59

Table 3.30—Continued

Civilian Occupation	Number of U.S. Jobs	Median Wages	Education at Entry	Distance Metric
Sheriffs and deputy sheriffs (E5)**	638,810	$56,810	High school diploma	93
Intelligence analysts (E5)*				
Correctional officers and jailers (E5)	434,420	$39,780	High school diploma	85
Fish and game wardens (E5)	5,820	$50,880	Bachelor's degree	78
Training and development specialists (E6)	239,500	$57,340	Bachelor's degree	67
Social and community service managers (E6)	116,670	$62,740	Bachelor's degree	76
Fitness and wellness coordinators (E6)	241,000	$34,980	Bachelor's degree	67
Criminal investigators and special agents (E6)	108,720	$79,870	High school diploma	89
Probation officers and correctional treatment specialists (E6)	86,810	$49,060	Bachelor's degree	69
Training and development managers (E6)	29,870	$101,930	Bachelor's degree	71
Private detectives and investigators (E6)	26,880	$44,570	Associate's degree	71
Security management specialists (E6)*				
Police detectives (E6)	108,720	$79,870	High school diploma	89
Forensic science technicians (E6)	13,570	$55,360	Bachelor's degree	83
Retail loss prevention specialists (E7)*				
Loss prevention managers (E7)*				
Security managers (E7)*				
Emergency management directors (E8)	9,770	$64,360	Bachelor's degree	87

* Not listed in Standard Occupation Classification system.
**The Bureau of Labor Statistics lists police patrol officers and sheriffs and deputy sheriffs as a single occupation.
NOTE: Matches do not account for statistically similar occupational matches resulting from estimation variance.

tions, including two high-quality matches, require a bachelor's degree at entry.

Occupational Analysis for Intelligence Analyst (MOS 35F)

Based on the Army's description of MOS 35F, the primary tasks of an intelligence analyst are to receive and process information from multiple intelligence sources, conduct analysis, and produce and disseminate intelligence to support military decisionmaking and other Army processes. Soldiers in this MOS also establish and maintain databases, prepare and present intelligence reports, and give briefings at all levels (Department of the Army, 2008a). We use the O*NET surveys to characterize the KSAs and work attributes of military police for comparison with civilian occupations.

Top-Rated KSAs of Intelligence Analysts

Table 3.31 shows the top-rated occupation attributes of intelligence analysts, based on our survey data. Many are associated with soft skills, including oral and written communication, critical thinking, decisionmaking, and conscientiousness.

Best-Matching Civilian Occupations for Intelligence Analysts

We found a total of 256 civilian occupations that scored 80 or higher on our distance metric for intelligence analysts, although only about one-fifth of them (53) require less than a bachelor's degree at entry. Twenty-three are general matches that are also shared by four or more MOSs, while 30 are MOS-specific matches. The top ten general and MOS-specific matches, selected based on their combined rankings on the distance metric, job density in the U.S. economy, and median wages, are shown in Tables 3.32 and 3.33, respectively. Although some soldiers who have served as intelligence analysts may want to continue in the same profession in the federal government, they may also consider other options that are good fits for their KSAs, such as general and operational managers, vocational education teachers, or even real estate agents.

Table 3.31
Top-Rated Occupation Attributes for Intelligence Analysts (MOS 35F)

Knowledge	Skills	Abilities
Clerical (25.2)	Reading comprehension (23.1)	Oral comprehension (25.1)
English language (22.6)	Active listening (20.2)	Written comprehension (24.9)
Public safety and security (22.3)	Critical thinking (19.7)	Oral expression (23.8)
Geography (21.7)	Judgment and decisionmaking (19.6)	Deductive reasoning (23.7)
Education and Training (20.5)	Speaking (19.1)	Speech clarity (22.4)
Work Activities	**Work Context**	**Work Styles**
Analyzing data or information (29.9)	Face-to-face discussions (4.8)	Analytical thinking (5.0)
Making decisions and solving problems (29.1)	Indoors, environmentally controlled (4.8)	Attention to detail (5.0)
Processing information (25.0)	Electronic mail (4.6)	Leadership (4.9)
Updating and using relevant knowledge (22.2)	Contact with others (4.5)	Adaptability/flexibility (4.8)
Monitor processes, materials, or surroundings (23.6)	Importance of being exact or accurate (4.3)	Dependability (4.8)

NOTES: For KSAs and work activities, score in parentheses is the product of the average importance score (scale of 1 to 5) and the average level score (scale of 1 to 7); for work context and work styles, score in parentheses is on a scale of 1 to 5. Soft skills are shown in shaded cells.

While it may not seem obvious that being a general and operations manager is a good match for an intelligence analyst, we compare their top-rated occupation attributes in Table 3.34. There are strong overlaps in the skills, abilities, work context, and work styles of general and operations managers and intelligence analysts, with at least three attributes rated in the top five by intelligence analysts. The biggest potential gaps are in the knowledge attributes of mathematics and

Table 3.32
Top Ten General Occupational Matches for Intelligence Analysts (MOS 35F)

Civilian Occupation	Number of U.S. Jobs	Median Wages	Education at Entry	Distance Metric
Detectives and criminal investigators	108,720	$79,870	High school diploma	94
First-line supervisors of police and detectives	101,420	$80,930	High school diploma	92
First-line supervisors of transportation and material-moving machine and vehicle operators	197,000	$54,930	High school diploma	89
Police and sheriff's patrol officers	638,810	$56,810	High school diploma	89
Respiratory therapists	119,410	$56,730	Associate's degree	88
Registered nurses	2,687,310	$66,640	Associate's degree	87
Correctional officers and jailers	434,420	$39,780	High school diploma	87
Transportation inspectors	24,350	$69,170	Postsecondary certification	86
Telecommunications equipment installers and repairers, except line installers	213,620	$55,190	Postsecondary certification	86
First-line supervisors of construction trades and extraction workers	496,370	$60,990	High school diploma	85

NOTE: Matches do not account for statistically similar occupational matches resulting from estimation variance.

economics and accounting and in managerial work activities, such as coordinating the work and activities of others, monitoring and controlling resources, and scheduling work and activities.

Table 3.33
Top Ten MOS-Specific Occupational Matches for Intelligence Analysts (MOS 35F)

Civilian Occupation	Number of U.S. Jobs	Median Wages	Education at Entry	Distance Metric
General and operations managers	2,049,870	97,270	Associate's degree	89
Power distributors and dispatchers	11,180	78,240	Associate's degree	86
Real estate sales agents	157,660	40,990	High school diploma	85
Vocational education teachers, postsecondary	121,200	48,360	Postsecondary certification	85
Police, fire, and ambulance dispatchers	96,390	37,410	High school diploma	85
Postmasters and mail superintendents	17,930	65,800	High school diploma	85
Industrial engineering technicians	65,680	53,370	Associate's degree	85
Wholesale and retail buyers, except farm products	110,560	52,270	Some college	83
Diagnostic medical sonographers	59,760	67,530	Associate's degree	81
First-line supervisors of office and administrative support workers	1,404,070	50,780	High school diploma	81

NOTE: Matches do not account for statistically similar occupational matches resulting from estimation variance.

Table 3.34
Top-Rated Occupation Attributes for General and Operations Managers and Intelligence Analysts (MOS 35F) Ratings of Those Attributes

Knowledge (33 Questions)	Skills (35 Questions)	Abilities (52 Questions)
Administration and management (6)	Reading comprehension (1)	Oral comprehension (1)
Customer and personal service (8)	Critical thinking (3)	Oral expression (3)
Personnel and human resources (9)	Speaking (5)	Written expression (7)
Mathematics (23)	Monitoring (13)	Problem sensitivity (6)
Economics and accounting (27)	Coordination (12)	Written comprehension (2)
		Deductive reasoning (4)
		Speech clarity (5)
		Information ordering (10)

Work Activities (41 Questions)	Work Context (57 Questions)	Work Styles (16 Questions)
Coordinating the work and activities of others (30)	Telephone (10)	Dependability (5)
Making decisions and solving problems (2)	Freedom to make decisions (20)	Attention to detail (2)
Monitoring and controlling resources (31)	Structured versus unstructured work (9)	Leadership (3)
Scheduling work and activities (32)	Contact with others (4)	Self-control (7)
Organizing, planning, and prioritizing work (19)	Impact of decisions on co-workers or company results (14)	Initiative (9)
	Face-to-face discussions (1)	
	Indoors, environmentally controlled (2)	
	Frequency of decisionmaking (17)	

NOTES: Attributes are listed in the order they are ranked by general and operations managers. Rankings by intelligence analysts are shown in parentheses. Soft skills are shown in shaded cells.

Comparison of Survey Matches for Intelligence Analysts with My Next Move for Veterans

The occupations recommended for intelligence analysts by My Next Move for Veterans (shown in Table 3.35) include computer operators, executive assistants, radio operators, and security managers. Several of these occupations rate 80 or higher on our distance metric, but have relatively low job density and median wages or require a bachelor's degree or higher at entry. For example, note that the Department of Labor estimates that there are only 1,100 radio operator jobs in the

Table 3.35
Civilian Occupations Recommended by My Next Move for Veterans for Intelligence Analysts (MOS 35F)

Civilian Occupation	Number of U.S. Jobs	Median Wages	Education at Entry	Distance Metric
Computer operators (E3)	58,060	$39,590	Associate's degree	84
Executive secretaries and executive administrative assistants (E3)	713,730	$51,270	Some college	78
Security management specialists (E4)*				
Radio operators (E4)	1,100	$46,380	High school diploma	87
Security managers (E4)*				
Instructional coordinators (E5)	133,780	$48,550	Master's degree	93
Vocational education teachers, postsecondary (E5)	121,200	$48,360	Postsecondary certification	85
Technical writers (E6)	48,210	$69,030	Associate's degree	77
Intelligence analysts (E6)*				
Training and development specialists (E6)	239,500	$57,340	Bachelor's degree	88

* Not listed in Standard Occupation Classification system.
NOTE: Matches do not account for statistically similar occupational matches resulting from estimation variance.

U.S. economy. While My Next Move for Veterans suggests ten occupations for intelligence analysts, we found 53 occupations that are high-quality matches for intelligence analysts and require less than a bachelor's degree at entry.

Occupational Analysis for Health Care Specialists (MOS 68W)

Based on the Army's description of MOS 68W (Department of the Army, 2008a), health care specialists are primarily responsible for providing emergency medical treatment, limited primary care, and health protection and evacuation from a point of injury or illness. The job duties of a health care specialist include administering emergency medical treatment to battlefield casualties, assisting with outpatient and inpatient care and treatment, preparing blood samples for laboratory analysis, and preparing patients, operating rooms, equipment, and supplies for surgery. The O*NET surveys reveal additional KSAs and work attributes of health care specialists that can be compared with civilian occupations.

Top-Rated KSAs for Health Care Specialists

Table 3.36 shows the top-rated occupation attributes for health care specialists. Note that many of their top-rated attributes, particularly skills, abilities, work context, and work styles, are associated with soft skills. These attributes reflect a range of different soft skills, including oral and written communication, continuous learning, training others, decisionmaking, and interpersonal skills.

Best-Matching Civilian Occupations for Health Care Specialists

Based on our survey data, we found 54 high-quality matches for health care specialists that scored 80 or higher on our distance metric, including 41 occupations that require less than a bachelor's degree at entry. Thirty-five are general matches that are shared by at least four MOSs we analyzed. The remaining six are MOS-specific. The top ten general matches, selected based on their combined rankings on the distance

Table 3.36
Top-Rated Occupation Attributes for Health Care Specialists (MOS 68W)

Knowledge	Skills	Abilities
Medicine and dentistry (22.7)	Active Listening (22.4)	Oral expression (24.4)
Customer and personal service (22.2)	Judgment and decisionmaking (21.6)	Problem sensitivity (24.0)
Psychology (19.3)	Instructing (21.5)	Oral comprehension (22.9)
Biology (17.7)	Active learning (21.3)	Written comprehension (22.7)
Education and training (17.3)	Reading comprehension (2.01)	Memorization (22.5)
Work Activities	**Work Context**	**Work Styles**
Assisting and caring for others (26.1)	Face-to-Face discussions (4.8)	Attention to detail (4.8)
Updating and using relevant knowledge (22.7)	Contact with others (4.6)	Dependability (4.7)
Monitor processes, materials, or surroundings (20.9)	Work with work group or team (4.5)	Concern for others (4.5)
Identifying objects, actions, and events (20.8)	Responsible for others' health and safety (4.4)	Stress tolerance (4.5)
Performing general physical activities (19.7)	Time pressure (4.2)	Adaptability/flexibility (4.5)

NOTES: For KSAs and work activities, score in parentheses is the product of the average importance score (scale of 1 to 5) and average level score (scale of 1 to 7); for work context and work styles, score in parentheses is on a scale of 1 to 5. Soft skills are shown in shaded cells.

metric, job density in the U.S. economy, and median wages, are shown in Table 3.37. All six MOS-specific matches are shown in Table 3.38.

Next, we discuss in more detail the occupational attributes that health care specialists and registered nurses (RNs) have in common. RN is a good general match for four of the five operational support and force sustainment MOSs in our analysis (the exception was MOS 91B, wheeled vehicle mechanic). The duties of RNs include assessing patient health problems and needs, developing and implementing nursing care

Table 3.37
Top Ten General Occupational Matches for Health Care Specialists (MOS 68W)

Civilian Occupation	Number of U.S. Jobs	Median Wages	Education at Entry	Distance Metric
Firefighters	308,790	$45,970	High school diploma	93
First-line supervisors of fire fighting and prevention workers	59,870	$70,670	High school diploma	92
Captains, mates, and pilots of water vessels	30,690	$72,340	Postsecondary certification	88
Police and sheriff's patrol officers	638,810	$56,810	High school diploma	87
Registered nurses	2,687,310	$66,640	Associate's degree	87
Respiratory therapists	119,410	$56,730	Associate's degree	87
First-Line supervisors of police and detectives	101,420	$80,930	High school diploma	86
Detectives and criminal investigators	108,720	$79,870	High school diploma	85
First-line supervisors of mechanics, installers, and repairers	434,810	$62,150	High school diploma	84
First-line supervisors of construction trades and extraction workers	496,370	$60,990	High school diploma	83

NOTE: Matches do not account for statistically similar occupational matches resulting from estimation variance.

plans, maintaining medical records, and administering nursing care to ill, injured, convalescent, or disabled patients. In addition, RNs may advise patients on health maintenance and disease prevention or provide case management. Licensing or registration is required, but there are one-year certificate and one- to three-year diploma programs for soldiers who wish to become RNs and already have some core nursing competencies.

Table 3.38
MOS-Specific Occupational Matches for Health Care Specialists (MOS 68W)

Civilian Occupation	Number of U.S. Jobs	Median Wages	Education at Entry	Distance Metric
Surgical technologists	98,450	$43,350	Associate's degree	83
Diagnostic medical sonographers	59,760	$67,530	Associate's degree	82
Physical therapist assistants	76,910	$54,410	Associate's degree	81
Magnetic resonance imaging technologists	33,130	$67,090	Associate's degree	80
Medical equipment preparers	50,550	$32,260	High school diploma	80
Chefs and head cooks	118,130	$41,610	Associate's degree	80

NOTE: Matches do not account for statistically similar occupational matches resulting from estimation variance.

RNs are a good match with operational support and force sustainment MOSs because they share some similar job characteristics. RNs often do shift work and sometimes work very long hours. Shift work is also common for these MOSs during deployments and in operational training environments. Both RNs and soldiers have to be able to react quickly to emergency situations and assess the situation upon arrival. RNs also learn a technical language or "codes" for medical conditions, as do soldiers such as unit supply specialists, who must learn a large number of supply status codes. RNs communicate to both patients and doctors about the patient's medical condition and are capable of speaking with technical vocabulary to medical professionals as well as speaking in lay terms with patients. Additionally, both soldiers and nurses are held accountable for equipment and supplies.

Like firefighters, RNs have been overlooked as high-quality matches by most military-civilian occupation crosswalks, despite the similarities noted above. For example, My Next Move for Veterans does not recommend RN as a match for any of the MOSs we analyzed, even for health care specialists. Yet, based on our occupation survey data, RN is one of the top matches for health care specialists, military police, intelligence analysts, and unit supply specialists.

In Table 3.39, we show the top-ranking job characteristics for RNs and compare them with those of health care specialists. Soft skills are shown in shaded cells. The number in parentheses after each attribute shows how health care specialists ranked these attributes. Many of the RNs' top-rated attributes were also rated in the top ten by health care specialists. There are particularly strong overlaps in knowledge, abilities, work activities, and work styles, with three or four of the RNs' top five attributes also rated in the top five by health care specialists. In addition, soft skills such as critical thinking, oral and written communication, conscientiousness, and dependability are important to both occupations. There are very few potential skill gaps; the largest discrepancy in ranking is speech recognition, which was ranked 7th by RNs and 34th by health care specialists.

Comparison of Survey Matches for Health Care Specialists with My Next Move for Veterans

In Table 3.40, we examine the occupations recommended by My Next Move for Veterans for health care specialists. We assess the match quality of each of these occupations using our distance metric. Our analysis suggests that the matches are quite varied. Emergency medical technician represents an excellent match with a score of 90 out of 100, but is not included in our top ten list of general matches because of relatively low median wages. However, medical secretaries seem to be very poor matches, with a score of 51 out of 100. All of the other matches fall below our cutoff of 80. Based on our analysis, other medical professions, such as RNs and surgical technicians, appear to be important omissions from the website.

Table 3.39
Top-Rated Occupation Attributes for Registered Nurses and Health Care Specialists' (MOS 68W) Ratings of These Attributes

Knowledge (33 Questions)	Skills (35 Questions)	Abilities (52 Questions)
Psychology (3)	Social perceptiveness (8)	Problem sensitivity (2)
Customer and personal service (2)	Active listening (1)	Oral comprehension (3)
Medicine and dentistry (1)	Reading comprehension (5)	Oral expression (1)
English language (6)	Speaking (12)	Inductive reasoning (6)
Education and training (5)	Critical thinking (6)	Written comprehension (4)
		Deductive reasoning (10)
		Speech recognition (34)
		Speech clarity (11)
Work Activities (41 Questions)	**Work Context (57 Questions)**	**Work Styles (16 Questions)**
Assisting and caring for others (1)	Telephone (15)	Attention to detail (1)
Identifying objects, actions, and events (4)	Contact with others (2)	Integrity (6)
Updating and using relevant knowledge (2)	Indoors, environmentally controlled (24)	Cooperation (9)
Monitor processes, materials, or surroundings (3)	Importance of being exact or accurate (10)	Stress tolerance (4)
Making decisions and solving problems (12)	Exposed to disease or infections (21)	Dependability (2)
	Physical proximity (11)	
	Face-to-face discussions (1)	
	Frequency of decisionmaking (20)	

NOTES: Attributes are listed in the order they are ranked by registered nurses. Rankings by health care specialists are shown in parentheses. Soft skills are shown in shaded cells.

Table 3.40
Civilian Occupations Recommended by My Next Move for Veterans for Health Care Specialists (MOS 68W)

Civilian Occupation	Number of U.S. Jobs	Median Wages	Education at Entry	Distance Metric
Emergency medical technicians and paramedics (E2)	235,760	$31,700	Postsecondary certification	90
Medical secretaries (E3)	516,050	$32,240	Some college	51
Medical assistants (E4)	584,970	$29,960	Postsecondary certification	76
Phlebotomists (E4)	111,950	$30,670	Postsecondary certification	74
Medical records and health information technicians (E4)	184,740	$35,900	High school diploma	58
Health educators (E5)	57,020	$50,430	Bachelor's degree	63
Medical and health services managers (E6)	310,320	$92,810	Bachelor's degree	64

NOTE: Matches do not account for statistically similar occupational matches resulting from estimation variance.

Occupational Analysis of Wheeled Vehicle Repairer (MOS 91B)

Based on the Army's description of MOS 91B (Department of the Army, 2008a), a wheeled vehicle repairer is a mechanic who is primarily responsible for supervising and performing maintenance and recovery operations on wheeled vehicles and associated items, such as heavy wheeled vehicles and select armored vehicles. The primary job duties of the wheeled vehicle repairer are maintaining wheeled vehicles and their associated trailers and material handling equipment systems; inspecting, servicing, maintaining, repairing, replacement, adjusting, and testing wheeled vehicles and material handling equipment systems, subsystems, and components; servicing automotive electrical systems, including wiring harnesses and starting and charging systems; and performing wheeled vehicle recovery operations. We use the O*NET survey data to identify the KSAs and work attributes of wheeled vehicle mechanics for comparison with civilian occupations.

Top-Rated KSAs for Wheeled Vehicle Repairer

In Table 3.41, we describe the top-rated occupation attributes of wheeled vehicle repairers. In contrast to some of the other MOSs we analyzed, their soft skills focus more on analytical thinking and conscientiousness rather than communication.

Table 3.41
Top-Rated Occupation Attributes for Wheeled Vehicle Repairers (MOS 91B)

Knowledge	Skills	Abilities
Mechanical (24.6)	Troubleshooting (27.1)	Extent flexibility (23.3)
Education and training (17.9)	Equipment maintenance (25.0)	Selective attention (22.7)
Clerical (15.9)	Repairing (23.8)	Deductive reasoning (22.3)
Administration and management (14.5)	Installation (22.4)	Problem sensitivity (22.0)
Transportation (14.3)	Instructing (21.4)	Static strength (21.9)
Work Activities	**Work Context**	**Work Styles**
Repairing and maintaining mechanical equipment (20.2)	Outdoors, exposed to weather (4.8)	Attention to detail (4.4)
Operating vehicles, mechanized devices, or equipment (18.7)	Contact with Others (4.6)	Dependability (4.3)
Handling and moving objects (17.1)	Spend time using your hands to handle, control, or feel objects, tools, or controls (4.6)	Cooperation (4.1)
Making decisions and solving problems (15.6)	Exposed to contaminants (4.6)	Achievement/effort (4.1)
Organizing, planning, and prioritizing work (15.5)	Face-to-face discussions (4.5)	Initiative (4.1)

NOTES: For KSAs and work activities, score in parentheses is the product of the average importance score (scale of 1 to 5) and average level score (scale of 1 to 7); for work context and work styles, score in parentheses is on a scale of 1 to 5. Soft skills are shown in shaded cells.

Best-Matching Civilian Occupations for Wheeled Vehicle Repairers

We found a total of 95 high-quality matching civilian occupations for wheeled vehicle repairers that scored 80 or higher on our distance metric; all but two of them require less than a bachelor's degree at entry. Of these occupations, 50 were general matches shared by four or more MOSs, and 43 were MOS-specific matches. We list the top ten general and MOS-specific matches, selected based on their combined rankings on the distance metric, job density in the U.S. economy, and median wages, in Tables 3.42 and 3.43, respectively.

Table 3.42
Top Ten General Occupational Matches for Wheeled Vehicle Repairers (MOS 91B)

Civilian Occupation	Number of U.S. Jobs	Median Wages	Education at Entry	Distance Metric
Captains, mates, and pilots of water vessels	30,690	$72,340	Postsecondary certification	93
Heating, air conditioning, and refrigeration mechanics and installers	261,390	$44,630	Postsecondary certification	92
Automotive service technicians and mechanics	633,390	$37,120	Postsecondary certification	92
Chemical plant and system operators	37,490	$55,900	High school diploma	91
Firefighters	308,790	$45,970	High school diploma	89
Electricians	566,930	$51,110	Postsecondary certification	89
Plumbers, pipefitters, and steamfitters	372,570	$50,660	Postsecondary certification	89
First-line supervisors of mechanics, installers, and repairers	434,810	$62,150	High school diploma	89
Aircraft mechanics and service technicians	116,830	$56,990	Postsecondary certification	88
First-line supervisors of production and operating workers	592,830	$55,520	High school diploma	86

NOTE: Matches do not account for statistically similar occupational matches resulting from estimation variance.

Table 3.43
Top Ten MOS-Specific Occupational Matches for Wheeled Vehicle Repairers (MOS 91B)

Civilian Occupation	Number of U.S. Jobs	Median Wages	Education at Entry	Distance Metric
Mobile heavy equipment mechanics, except engines	119,280	$47,580	Postsecondary certification	92
Farm equipment mechanics and service technicians	35,320	$36,150	High school diploma	87
Rail-track laying and maintenance equipment operators	14,820	$51,840	High school diploma	86
Carpenters	617,060	$40,820	High school diploma	86
Computer-controlled machine tool operators, metal and plastic	148,040	$36,440	High school diploma	86
Industrial machinery mechanics	313,880	$48,630	Postsecondary certification	85
Electrical power-line installers and repairers	114,540	$65,930	Postsecondary certification	85
Paving, surfacing, and tamping equipment operators	54,940	$38,660	High school diploma	85
Railroad conductors and yardmasters	42,900	$54,770	High school diploma	84
Rail car repairers	20,080	$54,020	High school diploma	83

NOTE: Matches do not account for statistically similar occupational matches resulting from estimation variance.

We selected the civilian occupation of industrial machinery mechanic for a more detailed comparison with the occupation attributes of wheeled vehicle mechanics. This occupation requires postsecondary certification, but should be reasonably accessible to junior soldiers separating from the Regular Army. It also pays fairly well (median annual wages of $48,630), and there are a large number of such jobs in the U.S. economy (313,880). Industrial machinery mechanics repair, install, adjust, or maintain industrial production and processing machinery or refinery and pipeline distribution systems. This job excludes millwrights (who are primarily installers of heavy industrial machinery); mobile heavy equipment mechanics, except engines; and machinery maintenance workers, who perform only routine tasks. As Table 3.43 indicates, mobile heavy equipment mechanics are also a high-quality match for wheeled vehicle mechanics.

Table 3.44 shows a comparison of industrial machinery mechanics' top-rated occupation attributes with those of wheeled vehicle repairers. There are particularly strong overlaps in skills, work context, and work styles, with three or four of industrial machinery mechanics' top-rated attributes also rated in the top five by wheeled vehicle mechanics. There is less overlap in abilities, where industrial machinery mechanics rate physical and sensory abilities more highly than cognitive abilities, which were emphasized by wheeled vehicle mechanics. The largest gaps appear to be in attributes such as design (knowledge), quality control analysis (skills), freedom to make decisions, and importance of being exact or accurate (work context).

Comparison of Survey Matches for Wheeled Vehicle Repairers with My Next Move for Veterans

Table 3.45 shows the civilian occupations recommended for wheeled vehicle mechanics by My Next Move for Veterans. Based on our distance metric, 9 of these 14 recommended occupations are high-quality matches, but some do not appear in Tables 3.42 and 3.43 because they have relatively low median wages or prevalence in the U.S. economy. Moreover, our occupational analysis found a large number of additional occupations that would be a good fit for wheeled vehicle repairers, some related to maintenance, but also including other fields, such as construction trades and computer-controlled machine tool operators. Note that two of the lower-quality matches in Table 3.45 are not associated with maintenance, tractor-trailer truck drivers and general and operations managers.

Table 3.44
Top-Rated Occupation Attributes for Industrial Machinery Mechanics and Wheeled Vehicle Repairers' (MOS 91B) Ratings of These Attributes

Knowledge (33 Questions)	Skills (35 Questions)	Abilities (52 Questions)
Mechanical (1)	Repairing (3)	Manual dexterity (9)
Engineering and technology (9)	Equipment maintenance (2)	Reaction time (12)
Production and processing (8)	Operation monitoring (16)	Control precision (25)
Design (21)	Troubleshooting (1)	Multi-limb coordination (24)
Mathematics (12)	Quality control analysis (26)	Finger dexterity (8)
		Information ordering (13)
		Hearing sensitivity (15)
		Near vision (11)

Work Activities (41 Questions)	Work Context (57 Questions)	Work Styles (16 Questions)
Repairing and maintaining mechanical equipment (1)	Face-to-face discussions (5)	Dependability (2)
Handling and moving objects (3)	Wear common protective or safety equipment (22)	Attention to detail (1)
Controlling machines and processes (9)	Spend time standing (16)	Cooperation (3)
Performing general physical activities (6)	Spend time using your hands to handle, control, or feel objects, tools, or controls (3)	Analytical thinking (11)
Inspecting equipment, structures, or material (11)	Contact with others (2)	Initiative (5)
	Exposed to hazardous equipment (30)	
	Freedom to make decisions (31)	
	Importance of being exact or accurate (32)	

NOTES: Attributes are listed in the order they are ranked by industrial machinery mechanics. Rankings by wheeled vehicle repairers are shown in parentheses. Soft skills are shown in shaded cells.

Table 3.45
Civilian Occupations Recommended by My Next Move for Veterans for Wheeled Vehicle Repairers (MOS 91B)

Civilian Occupation	Number of U.S. Jobs	Median Wages	Education at Entry	Distance Metric
Bus and truck mechanics and diesel engine specialists (E4)	243,080	$43,630	High school diploma	90
Automotive specialty technicians (E5)	633,390	$37,120	Postsecondary certification	92
First-line supervisors of mechanics, installers, and repairers (E5)	434,810	$62,150	High school diploma	89
Outdoor power equipment and other small engine mechanics (E5)	29,220	$32,120	High school diploma	81
Helpers—installation, maintenance, and repair workers (E5)	126,980	$25,390	High school diploma	79
Electrical and electronics installers and repairers, transportation equipment (E5)	14,160	$56,000	Postsecondary certification	80
Electronic equipment installers and repairers, motor vehicles (E5)	11,460	$31,020	Postsecondary certification	87
First-line supervisors of transportation and material-moving machine and vehicle operators (E5)	197,000	$54,930	High school diploma	76
Mobile heavy equipment mechanics (E5)	119,280	$47,580	Postsecondary certification	92
Heavy and tractor-trailer truck drivers (E5)	1,625,290	$39,520	High school diploma	76
Automotive master mechanics (E6)	633,390	$37,120	Postsecondary certification	92
Maintenance and repair workers, general (E6)	1,282,920	$36,170	High school diploma	71
Transportation vehicle, equipment and systems inspectors (E6)	24,350	$69,170	Postsecondary certification	82
General and operations managers (E6)	2,049,870	$97,270	Associate's degree	63

NOTE: Matches do not account for statistically similar occupational matches resulting from estimation variance.

Occupational Analysis for Unit Supply Specialist (MOS 92Y)

According to the Army's description of MOS 92Y (Department of the Army, 2008a), a unit supply specialist supervises or performs duties involving request, receipt, storage, issue, accountability, and preservation of individual, organizational, installation, and expendable supplies and equipment. Unit supply specialists' job duties include operating unit-level computers and maintaining the automated supply system for accounting of organizational and installation supplies and equipment; securing and controlling unit weapons and ammunition; and maintaining the unit property book for accountability and reporting. The O*NET occupation surveys identify the KSAs and work attributes of unit supply specialists for comparison with civilian occupations

Top-Rated KSAs for Unit Supply Specialists

In Table 3.46, we describe the top-rated occupation attributes of unit supply specialists. Note that more than half of the highest-rated attributes are associated with soft skills, particularly focusing on oral and written comprehension and expression, active learning, and attention to detail. Other attributes related to soft skills include management activities such as organizing, planning, and prioritizing work.

Best-Matching Civilian Occupations for Unit Supply Specialists

Among the MOSs we analyzed, we found the largest number of high-quality matches that scored 80 or higher on our distance metric for unit supply specialists. There are a total of 363 matching occupations, about half of which (181) require less than a bachelor's degree at entry. These occupations included 49 general matches shared by at least four MOSs we analyzed, and 132 MOS-specific matches, including general and operations managers, executive secretaries and executive administrative assistants, and production, planning, and expediting clerks. The top ten general and MOS-specific matches, selected based on their combined rankings on the distance metric, job density in the U.S. economy, and median wages, are shown in Tables 3.47 and 3.48, respectively.

Table 3.46
Top-Rated Occupation Attributes for Unit Supply Specialists (MOS 92Y)

Knowledge	Skills	Abilities
Clerical (20.0)	Monitoring (18.7)	Oral comprehension (20.0)
Administration and management (17.3)	Time management (18.5)	Written comprehension (20.0)
English language (11.1)	Speaking (18.1)	Number facility (20.0)
Education and training (10.9)	Learning strategies (18.0)	Oral expression (18.9)
Computers and electronics (8.0)	Active learning (17.6)	Written expression (18.9)
Work Activities	**Work Context**	**Work Styles**
Organizing, planning, and prioritizing work (27.8)	Electronic mail (5.0)	Dependability (4.9)
Communicating with supervisors, peers, or subordinates (23.0)	Face-to-face discussions (5.0)	Attention to detail (4.9)
Judging the qualities of things, services, or people (21.7)	Telephone (4.9)	Stress tolerance (4.8)
Monitoring and controlling resources (21.6)	Contact with others (4.9)	Integrity (4.8)
Establishing and maintaining interpersonal relationships (21.3)	Indoors, environmentally controlled (4.8)	Initiative (4.4)

NOTES: For KSAs and work activities, score in parentheses is the product of the average importance score (scale of 1 to 5) and average level score (scale of 0 to 7); for work context and work styles, score in parentheses is on a scale of 1 to 5. Soft skills are shown in shaded cells.

Table 3.47
Top Ten General Occupational Matches for Unit Supply Specialists (MOS 92Y)

Civilian Occupation	Number of U.S. Jobs	Median Wages	Education at Entry	Distance Metric
First-line supervisors of transportation and material-moving machine and vehicle operators	197,000	$54,930	High school diploma	97
Detectives and criminal investigators	108,720	$79,870	High school diploma	95
First-line supervisors of police and detectives	101,420	$80,930	High school diploma	95
Food service managers	198,610	$48,560	Less than high school	94
Transportation inspectors	24,350	$69,170	Postsecondary certification	94
First-line supervisors of fire fighting and prevention workers	59,870	$70,670	High school diploma	93
First-line supervisors of construction trades and extraction workers	496,370	$60,990	High school diploma	91
First-line supervisors of production and operating workers	592,830	$55,520	High school diploma	90
Police and sheriff's patrol officers	638,810	$56,810	High school diploma	89
Registered nurses	2,687,310	$66,640	Associate's degree	85

NOTE: Matches do not account for statistically similar occupational matches resulting from estimation variance.

Table 3.48
Top Ten MOS-Specific Occupational Matches for Unit Supply Specialists (MOS 92Y)

Civilian Occupation	Number of U.S. Jobs	Median Wages	Education at Entry	Distance Metric
General and operations managers	2,049,870	$97,270	Associate's degree	94
Production, planning, and expediting clerks	297,050	$45,670	High school diploma	91
Chefs and head cooks	118,130	$41,610	Associate's degree	91
First-line supervisors of retail sales workers	1,199,770	$37,860	High school diploma	91
Dispatchers, except police, fire, and ambulance	190,330	$36,690	High school diploma	91
Executive secretaries and executive administrative assistants	713,730	$51,270	Some college	90
Industrial engineering technicians	65,680	$53,370	Associate's degree	90
Power plant operators	40,300	$70,070	Associate's degree	90
Wholesale and retail buyers, except farm products	110,560	$52,270	Some college	89
Electrical and electronics engineering technicians	137,040	$59,820	Associate's degree	87

NOTE: Matches do not account for statistically similar occupational matches resulting from estimation variance.

We examine the top-ranking MOS-specific match, general and operations managers, in greater detail.[4] The primary tasks for these managers are to plan, direct, or coordinate the operations of companies or public- and private-sector organizations. Duties and responsibilities include formulating policies, managing daily operations, and planning the use of materials and human resources, but they are considered too diverse and general in nature to be classified in any one functional area of management or administration, such as personnel, purchasing, or administrative services. There are more than 2 million general and operations managers in the U.S. economy, and their median pay is nearly $100,000.

In Table 3.49, we compare the top-rated occupation attributes of general and operations managers with those of unit supply specialists. The strongest overlaps are in abilities, work context, and work styles, where three or four of general and operations managers' top-rated attributes are also ranked in the top five by unit supply specialists. There are relatively few potential gaps. The most notable are coordinating the work and activities of others, freedom to make decisions, and structured versus unstructured work.

Comparison of Survey Matches for Unit Supply Specialists with My Next Move for Veterans

The occupations recommended for unit supply specialists by My Next Move for Veterans are shown in Table 3.50. They include some relatively low-paid occupations, such as packers and packagers, stock clerks, and order clerks. The U.S. Department of Labor estimates that these occupations have median annual wages of $31,000 or less, far less than military compensation or the U.S. median annual wage. Seven of the 11 occupations recommended by My Next Move for Veterans score 80 or higher on our distance metric, although three of these occupations typically require a bachelor's degree at entry. The others do not appear in Tables 3.47 and 3.48 because of relatively low median wages. Based

---

[4] Recall that we also compared the occupation attributes of general and operations managers with intelligence analysts (MOS 35F). In that case, the distance metric was 89, so unit supply specialists are a slightly closer match. The types of overlapping attributes are also somewhat different.

Table 3.49
Top-Rated Occupation Attributes for General and Operations Managers and Unit Supply Specialists' (MOS 92Y) Ratings of Those Attributes

Knowledge (33 Questions)	Skills (35 Questions)	Abilities (52 Questions)
Administration and management (2)	Reading comprehension (8)	Oral comprehension (1)
Customer and personal service (8)	Critical thinking (13)	Oral expression (4)
Personnel and human resources (13)	Speaking (3)	Written expression (5)
Mathematics (10)	Monitoring (1)	Problem sensitivity (11)
Economics and accounting (6)	Coordination (7)	Written comprehension (2)
		Deductive reasoning (10)
		Speech clarity (18)
		Information ordering (8)
Work Activities (41 Questions)	**Work Context (57 Questions)**	**Work Styles (16 Questions)**
Coordinating the work and activities of others (36)	Telephone (3)	Dependability (1)
Making decisions and solving problems (6)	Freedom to make decisions (25)	Attention to detail (2)
Monitoring and controlling resources (4)	Structured versus unstructured work (21)	Leadership (10)
Scheduling work and activities (20)	Contact with others (4)	Self-control (8)
Organizing, planning, and prioritizing work (1)	Impact of decisions on co-workers or company results (14)	Initiative (5)
	Face-to-face discussions (2)	
	Indoors, environmentally controlled (5)	
	Frequency of decisionmaking (15)	

NOTES: Attributes are listed in the order they are ranked by general and operations managers. Rankings by unit supply specialists are shown in parentheses. Soft skills are shown in shaded cells.

Table 3.50
Civilian Occupations Recommended by My Next Move for Veterans for Unit Supply Specialists (MOS 92Y)

Civilian Occupation	Number of U.S. Jobs	Median Wages	Education at Entry	Distance Metric
Packers and packagers, hand (E3)	693,170	$20,330	High school diploma	72
Stock clerks—stockroom, warehouse, or storage yard (E3)	1,878,860	$22,850	High school diploma	75
Shipping, receiving, and traffic clerks (E3)	661,530	$29,930	High school diploma	92
Order clerks (E3)	190,390	$31,180	High school diploma	80
Laborers and freight, stock, and material movers, hand (E3)	2,400,490	$24,430	High school diploma	70
Bookkeeping, accounting, and auditing clerks (E3)	1,575,060	$36,430	High school diploma	86
Stock clerks, sales floor (E3)	1,878,860	$22,850	High school diploma	75
Purchasing agents (E4)	288,430	$60,980	Bachelor's degree	92
First-line supervisors of helpers, laborers, and material movers, hand (E5)	171,720	$46,690	High school diploma	95
Wholesale and retail buyers (E6)	1,394,640	$55,020	Bachelor's degree	88
Purchasing managers (E7)	70,840	$106,090	Bachelor's degree	90

NOTE: Matches do not account for statistically similar occupational matches resulting from estimation variance.

on our survey analysis, there is a much wider range of occupations that would be good fits for unit supply specialists.

Conclusions and Recommendations

Administering the O*NET occupation survey to enlisted AC soldiers and the subsequent data analysis indicates that this methodology is valuable in helping soldiers identify the KSAs they developed in the Army and communicate them to potential employers. It also identifies a wider range of civilian occupations than those that are recommended by existing military-civilian occupation crosswalks. One explanation for the improvement over existing crosswalks is the richness of the data provided by the O*NET surveys. For example, our analysis suggests that even highly developed existing crosswalks do not address the key issue of soft skills as well as the O*NET surveys can.

The Army should consider developing materials that communicate the occupation survey results both to transitioning soldiers and potential employers, to help them better understand the KSAs that soldiers develop during their Army careers. These results could also help soldiers translate their KSAs into civilian terms in job interviews and other interactions with potential employers. The Army might consider implementing the occupation surveys online to collect larger samples of data by pay grade and to extend the analysis to additional MOSs. The occupation surveys could also potentially be incorporated into the transition counseling process to develop occupation matches tailored to the specific soldier's KSAs and interests.

In addition, information on the KSAs developed in different MOSs could even be used in recruiting or to channel recruits into MOSs that would help them prepare for their desired civilian careers after separating from the Army.

CHAPTER FOUR

General Matches with Soldier Skills

As Chapter Three shows, we found that many occupations matched well with four or more of the ten MOSs we analyzed. In this chapter, we discuss these general matches and the reasons why they recur in multiple MOSs. Table 4.1 lists all of the civilian occupations that scored 80 or higher on our distance metric for seven or more of the ten MOSs we analyzed. In Appendix D, Table D.1, we list all 66 of the civilian occupations that are good matches for at least four of the ten MOSs.

Why are there so many civilian occupations that are high-quality matches for multiple Army MOSs? One explanation is that all soldiers share a common set of core KSAs. The *Soldier's Manual of Common Tasks* (Department of the Army, 2015, and 2008b) describes the individual-level tasks in which *all* soldiers are required to be proficient. These tasks include proficiency in individual-assigned weapon (rifle, pistol, etc.), individual and team movement on the battlefield, communicating through radios, vocal commands, hand and arm signals, first aid, reacting to enemy actions, and understanding and reacting to evolving situations.

In addition to the military-specific expertise each soldier develops, there are other characteristics and attributes that are taught to soldiers as part of being an Army professional. These Army values then become part of each soldier's core values: loyalty, duty, respect, selfless service, honor, integrity, and personal courage. Much of the Army's culture of duty, loyalty, and responsibility is clearly reflected in soldiers' rankings of their own soft skills (see Appendix A).

Table 4.1
Civilian Occupations that Match with Seven or More MOSs

Civilian Occupation	Number of Matches
First-line supervisors of fire fighting and prevention workers	10
Ship engineers	10
First-line supervisors of mechanics, installers, and repairers	9
Firefighters	9
Captains, mates, and pilots of water vessels	9
Fire inspectors and investigators	9
First-line supervisors of helpers, laborers, and material movers, hand	8
Aircraft mechanics and service technicians	8
Septic tank servicers and sewer pipe cleaners	8
First-line supervisors of farming, fishing, and forestry workers	8
Aircraft cargo handling supervisors	8
Police and sheriff's patrol officers	7
First-line supervisors of production and operating workers	7
First-line supervisors of construction trades and extraction workers	7
Telecommunications equipment installers and repairers, except line installers	7
Millwrights	7
Forest and conservation technicians	7
Transportation inspectors	7
Manufactured building and mobile home installers	7

NOTE: Matches do not account for statistically similar occupational matches resulting from estimation variance.

The O*NET surveys identify additional occupation attributes that are shared by many of the MOSs we analyzed.

Common Soldier KSAs

In Tables 4.2–4.7, we show the top-rated KSAs and work attributes and highlight in shaded cells those that are common across the ten MOSs we analyzed, underscoring the point that common soldier KSAs form the basis of many military-civilian occupational matches. For example, soldiers in five of the ten MOSs rated public safety and security as the most important or second most important knowledge area needed in

Table 4.2
Most Important Knowledge Attributes in Each MOS

MOS	Description	Most Important Attribute	Second Most Important Attribute
11B	Infantryman	Public safety and security	Geography
12B	Combat engineer	Engineering and technology	Geography
13B	Cannon crewmember	Education and training	Administration and management
19D	Cavalry scout	Geography	Public safety and security
19K	Armor crewman	Mechanical	Public safety and security
31B	Military police	Public safety and security	Customer and personal service
35F	Intelligence analyst	Clerical	Public safety and security
68W	Health care specialist	Medicine and dentistry	Customer and personal service
91B	Wheeled vehicle repairer	Mechanical	Education and training
92Y	Unit supply specialist	Clerical	Administration and management

their job. Other frequently occurring knowledge areas are geography and education and training.

In Table 4.3, we show the top-rated skills reported by each MOS. O*NET divides skills into two broad categories, content and process, so we show the top-rated skill in each category. As Table 4.3 indicates, soldiers in five of the ten MOSs reported that their top-rated content skill is active listening. Soldiers in three additional MOSs rated it as their second most important content skill. Soldiers in four of the ten MOSs rated equipment maintenance as their most important process skill, with soldiers in an additional two MOSs rating it as their second most important process skill.

Table 4.4 shows the top-rated abilities for each MOS, divided into the O*NET categories of cognitive abilities, psychomotor abilities, physical abilities, and sensory abilities. In each category, one ability was ranked highest by soldiers in three or four of the ten MOSs; additional MOSs that ranked that ability second highest are indicated by table notes.

Table 4.3
Most Important Content and Process Skills in Each MOS

MOS	Top-Rated Content Skill	Top-Rated Process Skill
11B	Critical thinking[a]	Equipment maintenance
12B	Mathematics[a]	Equipment maintenance
13B	Active listening	Equipment maintenance
19D	Active listening	Coordination[b]
19K	Active listening	Equipment maintenance
31B	Active listening	Persuasion
35F	Reading comprehension[a]	Judgment and decisionmaking
68W	Active listening	Instructing
91B	Monitoring	Troubleshooting[b]
92Y	Monitoring	Time management

[a] The second highest-rated content skill for this MOS is active listening

[b] The second highest-rated process skill for this MOS is equipment maintenance

Table 4.4
Most Important Cognitive, Psychomotor, Physical, and Sensory Abilities in Each MOS

MOS	Cognitive	Psychomotor	Physical	Sensory
11B	Selective attention	Stamina	Speed of limb movement	Night vision
12B	Problem sensitivity[a]	Explosive strength[b]	Speed of limb movement	Far vision
13B	Oral expression	Trunk strength	Rate control	Peripheral vision
19D	Selective attention	Static strength	Rate control[c]	Peripheral vision
19K	Selective attention	Static strength	Speed of limb movement	Peripheral vision
31B	Oral comprehension	Trunk strength	Speed of limb movement	Speech clarity
35F	Oral comprehension	Explosive strength	Wrist-finger speed	Visual color discrimination
68W	Oral expression	Static strength	Reaction time	Speech clarity
91B	Selective attention	Extent flexibility[b]	Manual dexterity	Depth perception
92Y	Number facility	Static strength	Finger dexterity	Depth perception

[a] The second highest-rated ability for this MOS is selective attention.

[b] The second highest-rated ability for this MOS is static strength.

[c] The second highest-rated ability for this MOS is speed of limb movement.

Table 4.5 shows the highest-rated work activities for each MOS. We found that four of the five maneuver, fires, and effects MOSs rated performing general physical activities as their most important work activity, but otherwise, there was very little commonality among the top two work activities of the ten MOSs.

Table 4.6 shows the highest-rated work context attributes for each MOS, divided into the O*NET categories of interpersonal relationships, physical work conditions, and structural job characteristics. We find a very high degree of commonality in the three work context categories, which are typically expressed as either frequency or importance of the attribute. Six of the ten MOSs ranked face-to-face discussions with individuals or teams as the most frequent interpersonal

Table 4.5
Most Important Work Activities in Each MOS

MOS	Most Important Work Activity	Second Most Important Work Activity
11B	Performing general physical activities	Making decisions and solving problems
12B	Performing general physical activities	Identifying objects, actions, and events
13B	Training and teaching others	Coaching and developing others
19D	Performing general physical activities	Handling and moving objects
19K	Performing general physical activities	Handling and moving objects
31B	Performing for or working directly with the public	Resolving conflicts and negotiating with others
35F	Analyzing data or information	Making decisions and solving problems
68W	Assisting and caring for others	Updating and using relevant knowledge
91B	Repairing and maintaining mechanical equipment	Operating vehicles, mechanized devices, or equipment
92Y	Organizing, planning, and prioritizing work	Communicating with supervisors, peers, or subordinates

relationship attribute, and three of the remaining MOSs ranked it as the second most frequently occurring attribute in this category. Contact with others was also rated as the second most frequent attribute by five MOSs (12B, 13B, 19D, 31B, and 68W). Eight of the ten MOSs ranked working outdoors, exposed to all weather conditions, as their most frequent physical work condition; the two exceptions were intelligence analysts (35F) and unit supply specialists (92Y). Seven of the ten MOSs ranked time pressure as the most important structural job characteristic, with one additional MOS ranking it as the second most important. In addition, the importance of being exact or accurate was ranked as the second highest attribute by four MOSs (11B, 19D, 31B,

Table 4.6
Most Important Work Context Attributes in Each MOS

MOS	Most Frequent Interpersonal Relationship Attribute	Most Frequent Physical Work Condition Attribute	Most Important Structural Job Characteristic
11B	Contact with others	Outdoors, exposed to weather	Time pressure
12B	Face-to-face discussions	Outdoors, exposed to weather	Time pressure
13B	Face-to-face discussions	Outdoors, exposed to weather	Importance of being exact or accurate
19D	Face-to-face discussions	Outdoors, exposed to weather	Time pressure
19K	Contact with others[a]	Outdoors, exposed to weather	Time pressure
31B	Face-to-face discussions	Outdoors, exposed to weather	Time pressure
35F	Face-to-face discussions	Indoors, environmentally controlled	Importance of being exact or accurate[b]
68W	Face-to-face discussions	Outdoors, exposed to weather	Time pressure
91B	Contact with others[a]	Outdoors, exposed to weather	Time pressure
92Y	Electronic mail[a]	Indoors, environmentally controlled	Consequence of error

[a] The second most frequent interpersonal relationship attribute for this MOS is face-to-face discussions

[b] The second most important structural job charactertistic for this MOS is time pressure.

and 92Y), and consequence of error[1] was ranked as the second highest attribute by three MOSs (12B, 68W, and 91B).

Table 4.7 shows the work style attributes ranked most important and second most important by each MOS. The most frequently occurring attribute is attention to detail, which was ranked highest by five MOSs and second highest by three MOSs.

One consequence of these common soldier KSAs and work attributes is that there is a common set of civilian occupations that capitalize on the same attributes and thus are good matches for several MOSs. Of the 66 civilian occupations that were good matches with at least four MOSs—evidence of a general match with common soldier KSAs—very few require more than a high school degree or a postsecondary certification at entry (note that we restricted these matches to require less than a bachelor's degree). Although soldiers in the MOSs we analyzed are unlikely to have training or certifications in areas such

Table 4.7
Most Important Work Style Attributes in Each MOS

MOS	Most Important Work Style Attribute	Second Most Important Work Style Attribute
11B	Stress tolerance	Attention to detail
12B	Attention to detail	Leadership
13B	Achievement/effort	Attention to detail
19D	Leadership	Stress tolerance
19K	Attention to detail	Leadership
31B	Integrity	Self-control
35F	Attention to detail	Analytical thinking
68W	Attention to detail	Dependability
91B	Attention to detail	Dependability
92Y	Dependability	Attention to detail

[1] This question is phrased as "How serious would the result usually be if the worker made a mistake that was not readily correctable?"

as sheet metal work or electronics repair, the survey results suggest that soldiers possess other nontechnical skills that make them well suited to the types of occupations listed in Table 4.1 and additional general matches shown in Appendix D, Table D.1. In particular, there are a number of first-line supervisory positions that emphasize initiative, communication, conflict resolution, and focus on process analysis, data use, and performance evaluation. In every Army MOS, soldiers are expected to develop skills such as these in order to progress to higher ranks.

One of the most frequent military-civilian occupational matches in our analysis is firefighter. In nine of the ten MOSs we analyzed—the exception being intelligence analyst (35F)—firefighter was among the top high-quality matches (in most cases, it was the top match or the second-best match, based on the distance metric). There are a number of reasons for this outcome: Firefighting requires individual and team movement, navigation through unknown environments, proficiency with equipment, communications with both hand signals and by radio, strength, fitness, and an ethos of duty and responsibility.

It is surprising that other occupation crosswalks have overlooked firefighting as a high-quality match, despite its obvious similarities with soldier duties. For example, My Next Move for Veterans does not recommend firefighter for any of the MOSs we analyzed. Yet, based on our occupational survey data, firefighter is *the* best match strictly using the distance measure for four of ten MOSs, and also the best overall match considering other factors such as job density and entry-level qualifications. One possible explanation is that the O*NET surveys are better able to account for the importance of soft skills (e.g., teamwork) in making occupation matches in a way that other translators cannot. For example, one particularly salient point on the quality of the match is the role of close-knit teamwork when fighting a fire. Clear communication is essential, but so is coordination between different members of the firefighting team. Contrast this with the most often recommended occupation for soldiers—police work. Police officers generally work independently or in two- or three-person teams. Only occasionally are police officers required to coordinate large team actions.

We list additional general matches in Appendix D. While we do not discuss each of these matches in detail, we did find some broad themes. Of the 66 occupations that were good matches with four or more of the ten MOSs we analyzed, approximately 30 percent were construction and extraction occupations (sheet metal workers, mining machine operators), nearly 20 percent were installation, maintenance, and repair occupations (electrical and electronics repair, bus and truck mechanics), another 20 percent were manufacturing occupations (first-line supervisors of production and operating workers), and 15 percent were protective service occupations (such as firefighters and police officers).

CHAPTER FIVE

Findings and Recommendations

Findings

The civilian occupation surveys generated a rich database of the KSAs needed by Army soldiers to perform ten of the largest Army MOSs, accounting for about 40 percent of all AC enlisted personnel. These data allowed us to identify both a broader range of civilian occupations that utilize KSAs developed in the Army and higher-quality matches than existing military-civilian occupation crosswalks. The best-matching civilian occupations included some that made use of common soldier KSAs that were shared by multiple MOSs we analyzed, as well as others that utilized MOS-specific KSAs. Our analysis also revealed that some occupations recommended by existing crosswalks, such as My Next Move for Veterans, do not match very well with the KSAs of the MOSs we analyzed. In part, this occurred because these poorly matching occupations do not make use of soft skills developed in the Army, such as teamwork, leadership, and training, coaching, and mentoring others.

Recommendations

There are a number of ways the Army can make use of our occupation survey data and analysis. First, the Army should provide information on the best civilian job matches to transitioning soldiers in the ten MOSs we analyzed. This information should include the types of employers they should target, the KSAs they should emphasize in their discussions with employers, and potential skill gaps or credentials they may need. Second, the Army should also develop a communication plan for employers in these occupations, identifying which MOSs are good matches for them and the KSAs these soldiers have developed in the Army. In addition, the Army should provide information to employers about the number of soldiers in these MOSs leaving the Regular Army each year and their planned geographic locations. These recommendations are limited to the MOSs for which we have sufficient data; having additional data for other MOSs would improve this communication plan.

Therefore, we recommend that the Army expand use of the occupation surveys to develop crosswalks for additional MOSs. The Department of Labor has already implemented online versions of the surveys to collect data on civilian occupations. Making the surveys available to soldiers online, and integrating them into the Transition Assistance Program, is one option for expanding their use and would greatly increase the amount of data available to analyze the best civilian occupation matches by MOS and pay grade; an online format could even help generate job recommendations for individual soldiers based on their own survey responses and would allow them to identify their own KSA gaps for other civilian occupations they may wish to pursue.

APPENDIX A

Soft Skills in Army Occupations

How Can Soft Skills Be Defined?

To identify and define soft skills (or, more broadly, essential nontechnical skills), we began with a list developed by Hardison et al. (2015) in a similar military context. That list drew from a number of sources, most notably from the considerable existing literature on competencies and from established sources of such lists, including the U.S. Department of Labor, the U.S. Office of Personnel Management, and the National Academy of Sciences. In reviewing this list, we also felt that two soft skills could be usefully added—adaptability and integrity. Table A.1 contains the full list of 18 soft skills, further grouped into five broad categories. For example, in the first grouping, "decisionmaking" and "critical thinking" are both cognitive skills, and, in the second grouping "continuous learning" and "training others" are both about learning.

Once the soft skills were identified, we further defined them by matching them with O*NET survey questions (see Table A.2).[1] This process was far from perfect, as the O*NET surveys were not originally designed to define soft skills. In some instances, these matches were simple and straightforward; for example, the O*NET question on dependability, defined as "job requires being reliable, responsible and dependable, and fulfilling obligations" could be directly connected

[1] Note the difference in terminology used in the two sources. In particular, in the "Soft Skill" list, all attributes are referred to as "skills"; whereas the O*NET questions are referred to by six different names: knowledge, skills, abilities, work activities, work context, and work styles.

Table A.1
Soft Skills List and Titles

Area	Soft Skill Title
Cognitive	• Decisionmaking/decisiveness • Critical thinking
Learning	• Continuous learning • Training others
Interpersonal	• Teamwork and teambuilding • Interpersonal skills • Oral communication • Written communication • Adaptability
Intrapersonal	• Operating safely • Handling work stress • Being dependable and reliable • Conscientiousness/attention to detail • Persistence • Integrity
Managing	• Project planning • Leading, motivating, and inspiring others • Managing and supervising

SOURCE: Derived from Hardison et al., 2015.

with "being dependable and reliable" in the soft skills list. In other instances, the match was more complex; for example, "interpersonal skills" was linked to questions in the O*NET surveys about social perceptiveness, service orientation, social orientation, concern for others, and establishing and maintaining interpersonal relationships. Moreover, in a few instances, O*NET survey items were connected to more than one skill. For example, the skill of "complex problem solving" is related to both "decisionmaking" and "critical thinking" in the soft skill list.

Finally, it is worth noting that survey items were not included in the definition of soft skills unless they were considered an essential element of the definitions. It was not enough for a question to simply be related to a particular skill; it also had to apply in most situations. For example, while the ability of "mathematical reasoning" is related to the soft skill "critical thinking," it was not included because there are many ways to be a critical thinker without mastering mathemati-

Table A.2
Soft Skill and O*NET Survey Question Crosswalk

Soft Skill	O*NET Reference	O*NET Survey Item
Decisionmaking/ decisiveness	• SK17 • SK31 • WA10A • WC48	• Complex problem solving • Judgment and decisionmaking • Making decisions and solving problems • Freedom to make decisions
Critical thinking	• AB7 • AB8 • AB9 • SK7 • SK17 • WS16	• Problem sensitivity • Deductive reasoning • Inductive Reasoning • Critical thinking • Complex problem solving • Analytical thinking
Teamwork and teambuilding	• WA34 • WC07 • WS05	• Developing and building teams • Work with work group or team • Cooperation
Continuous learning	• SK08 • SK09 • WA12	• Active learning • Learning strategies • Updating and using relevant knowledge
Training others	• KN23 • SK09 • SK15 • WA35 • WA37	• Education and training • Learning strategies • Instructing • Training and teaching others • Coaching and developing others
Interpersonal skills	• SK11 • SK16 • WA28 • WS06 • WS07	• Social perceptiveness • Service orientation • Establishing and maintaining personal relationships • Concern for others • Social orientation
Oral communication	• AB01 • AB03 • AB51 • AB52 • SK04 • SK13 • WA26 • WC01 • WC02	• Oral comprehension • Oral expression • Speech recognition • Speech clarity • Speaking • Persuasion • Communicating with supervisors/peers/ subordinates • Face-to-face discussions • Public speaking

Table A.2—Continued

Soft Skill	O*NET Reference	O*NET Survey Item
Written communication	• AB02 • AB04 • SK01 • SK03 • WA26 • WC05	• Written comprehension • Written expression • Reading comprehension • Writing • Communicating with supervisors/peers/ subordinates • Writing letters and memos
Adaptability	• WS10	• Adaptability/flexibility
Operating safely	• WC10	• Responsible for health and safety of others
Handling work stress	• WC45 • WS09	• Consequence of error • Stress tolerance
Being dependable and reliable	• WS11	• Dependability
Conscientiousness/ attention to detail	• AB17 • AB20 • SK10 • WC50 • WS12	• Perceptual speed • Selective attention • Monitoring • Importance of being exact or accurate • Attention to detail
Persistence	• WS01 • WS02	• Achievement/effort • Persistence
Integrity	• WS13	• Integrity
Project planning	• WA15	• Organizing, planning, and prioritizing work
Leading, motivating, and inspiring others	• WA36 • WS04	• Guiding, directing, and motivating subordinates • Leadership
Managing and supervising	• SK10 • WA33 • WA37 • WC09 • WC11	• Monitoring • Coordinating the work and activities of others • Coaching and developing others • Coordinate or lead others in work activities • Responsible for work outcomes and results

NOTES: In the O*Net references, KN refers to the Knowledge module; SK to the Skills module; AB to the Abilities module; WA to the Work Activities module; WC to the Work Context module; and WS to the Work Styles module of the O*NET. The number refers to the question number in the respective survey.

cal skills. Furthermore, while "management of financial resources" is related to the soft skill "project planning," the item was not included under that definition because it is possible to be highly involved in such planning without managing finances. In all, 58 of the O*NET attributes (or 25 percent of all attributes used in our analysis) were used to define soft skills.

How Is the Importance of Soft Skills Measured?

To measure the relative importance of the various soft skills in Army occupations, we averaged the importance scores (ranging from 1 to 5) across all individuals and subcomponents of the soft skill category. The soft skill "leading, motivating, and inspiring others" can serve as an example, shown to be connected to two O*NET survey questions in Table A.2. If, in the survey, an Army enlisted member rated the importance of "guiding, directing, and motivating subordinates" as a 3 (important) and "Leadership" as a 5 (extremely important), the score for the soft skill "Leading, motivating, and inspiring others" would be the average, or 4.00. Note that, at the extreme (for the skill "oral communication"), we were averaging responses to nine survey questions to get a score on the soft skill.

How Important Are Soft Skills Across Army Occupations?

In Table A.3, we show the average score on each soft skill over all responders for all ten MOSs surveyed in this project. All soft skills averaged at least "important"; that is, for every MOS, every soft skill averaged above a 3.00. Overall, soldiers see soft skills in their occupation as being "very important" (i.e., average rating was 3.98).

Across all soft skills, Table A.3 shows that "being dependable and reliable" was rated the highest among soft skills (average rating 4.55). Interpersonal skills, while still important, were rated the lowest (average rating more than 1 point lower at 3.48). Figure A.1 shows the variation in average rating across the different soft skills for all survey respon-

Table A.3
Average Soft Skill Importance Scores, by Army MOS

Soft Skill	11B	12B	13B	19D	19K	31B	35F	68W	91B	92Y	Avg.
Decisionmaking/decisiveness	3.76	3.73	3.44	3.41	3.80	3.76	389	3.76	3.71	3.68	3.69
Critical thinking	3.95	3.78	3.78	3.64	3.79	3.87	4.37	4.14	3.93	3.36	3.86
Continuous learning	3.84	3.78	3.70	3.47	3.88	3.90	3.88	3.99	3.68	3.80	3.79
Training others	4.03	3.75	3.92	3.51	3.92	3.87	3.40	3.79	3.65	3.77	3.76
Teamwork and teambuilding	4.50	4.23	4.30	4.17	4.34	4.34	3.85	4.13	3.98	4.00	4.18
Interpersonal skills	3.68	3.43	3.02	3.34	3.65	3.85	3.38	3.87	3.24	3.33	3.48
Oral communication	4.03	3.63	3.64	3.73	3.80	4.10	4.03	3.94	3.50	3.57	3.80
Written communication	3.38	3.35	3.46	3.49	3.35	4.03	4.26	3.86	3.41	4.14	3.67
Adaptability	4.72	4.48	4.38	4.53	4.76	4.63	4.75	4.53	4.00	4.33	4.51
Operating safely	4.31	4.06	4.11	3.80	4.07	4.35	3,50	4.35	3.75	4.13	4.04
Handling work stress	4.26	4.02	4.14	4.18	4.13	3.99	3.81	4.32	3.97	4.64	4.15
Being dependable and reliable	4.72	4.22	4.50	4.47	4.76	4.19	4.75	4.68	4.33	4.89	4.55
Conscientiousness/attention to detail	4.14	3.74	4.09	3.91	3.93	3.81	3.99	4.13	3.59	3.71	3.90
Persistence	4.15	3.94	4.50	4.16	4.35	3.90	4.31	4.18	4.00	3.50	4.10
Integrity	4.69	4.21	4.00	4.32	4.76	4.81	4.75	4.47	3.56	4.78	4.44
Project planning	3.58	4.13	3.11	3.68	3.83	4.11	3.13	3.55	3.63	4.50	3.72
Leading, motivating, and inspiring others	4.40	4.34	4.07	4.22	4.61	4.51	3.88	3.91	3.75	3.94	4.16
Managing and supervising	4.02	3.81	3.89	3.66	3.78	4.05	3.20	3.58	3.67	3.93	3.76
Average of all soft skills	4.12	3.92	3.89	3.87	4.08	4.12	3.95	4.07	3.74	4.00	3.98

NOTE: Scale is 1 (not important); 2 (somewhat important); 3 (important); 4 (very important); and 5 (extremely important).

Figure A.1
Average Soft Skill Importance Rating, by Individual Soft Skill

RAND *RR1719-A.1*

dents. Notice that the top three skills—being dependable and reliable, adaptability, and integrity—are all halfway between "very important" and "extremely important" and significantly above other soft skill ratings. Other skills that average above 4.0 across all MOSs are leadership, teamwork, handling work stress, and operating safely.

This is not to say that all soldiers within an MOS have a job that gives them the same experience, even if the overall average is high. For example, while "adaptability" had a 4.5 average, the second-highest soft skill, a few soldiers rated the skill as either not important or only somewhat important in their particular job.

What Is the "Most Important" Soft Skill, and How Does That Vary by MOS?

The determination of the single soft skill that was "most important" for a particular MOS was complicated by the similarities of ratings among skills within an MOS. For example, while one particular skill may have the highest average rating within an MOS, the difference between that rating and the second-highest (or even third- or fourth-highest) rating was often not significant in a sense. Thus, to examine the variation in the most important skill by MOS, we included the skill with the highest average *plus* any other skill that did not have a significantly different mean.

Our first finding was that some soft skills were highly rated across all MOSs in our study. These included four soft skills:

- being dependable and reliable
- adaptability
- integrity
- operating safely.

That some skills have the highest rating in Army work life regardless of occupation is consistent with Army values and training.

Next, we identified skills that were highly rated in some MOSs but not in others. As shown in Table A.4, nine additional soft skills were given the highest rating (after the four identified above) in at least one MOS.[2] Note that the maneuver, fires, and effects occupations—combat arms occupations (the first five columns of the table)—tend to have different top-rated skills than the operational support and force sustainment occupations (shown in the last five columns). Overall,

[2] Five of the soft skills, while always considered important, were never given the highest rating within an MOS: oral communication, continuous learning, managing and supervising, training others, and interpersonal skills.

Table A.4
Soft Skills Rated as Most Important by a Subset of MOSs

Soft Skill	11B	12B	13B	19D	19K	31B	35F	68W	91B	92Y
Leading, motivating, and inspiring others	X	X	X	X	X	X			X	
Teamwork and teambuilding	X	X	X	X		X		X	X	
Project planning		X		X		X			X	X
Handling work stress			X	X				X	X	X
Persistence			X	X			X	X	X	
Critical thinking							X	X	X	
Written communication							X			
Conscientiousness/ attention to detail								X		
Decisionmaking/ decisiveness									X	

NOTE: Table excludes the four soft skills (being dependable and reliable; adaptability; integrity; operating safely) that are top-rated in all ten MOSs.

"leading, motivating, and inspiring others" as well as "teamwork and team building" were among the most important for seven of the ten MOSs, especially in maneuver, fires and effects MOSs. Project planning, persistence, and handling work stress are top in five MOSs spread across both MOS groups. Critical thinking was rated among the most important soft skills in three MOSs: intelligence analyst (35F), health care specialist (68W), and wheeled vehicle repairer (91B). Finally, decisionmaking, written communication, and attention to detail are top-rated in one MOS each.

How Do Importance Ratings of Soft Skills Vary by Pay Grade?

The importance of soft skills is likely to vary by pay grade, given that enlisted personnel take on different jobs and greater responsibilities as they advance in rank. While sample sizes in this study were generally too small to study soft skill importance at that level of detail, we were able to compare importance ratings for E1–E4s versus E5–E9s for 11Bs, where we had a considerably larger sample size. The results are shown in Table A.5.

Table A.5
Mean Importance Ratings in MOS 11B for E1–E4s Compared with E5–E9s

Soft Skill	E1–E4	E5–E9
Decisionmaking/decisiveness	3.43	4.38
Critical thinking	3.84	4.17
Continuous learning	3.69	4.14
Training others	3.78	4.56
Teamwork and teambuilding	4.39	4.70
Interpersonal skills	3.51	4.12
Oral communication	3.89	4.30
Written communication	2.87	3.95
Operating safely	4.04	4.91
Handling work stress	4.25	4.32
Being dependable and reliable	4.66	5.00
Attention to detail/conscientiousness	4.12	4.27
Persistence	4.12	4.29
Project planning	3.20	4.15
Leading, motivating, and inspiring others	4.17	4.85
Managing and Supervising	3.75	4.52
Adaptability	4.69	4.86
Integrity	4.62	5.00
Overall average	3.95	4.47

Overall, the average importance rating is more than half a point higher for E5–E9s (4.47) than for E1–E4s (3.95), perhaps indicating the increased level of responsibility taken on by noncommissioned officers. However, while the rating goes up for the higher group for every skill, the difference is not always statistically significant. Some skills are of relatively equal importance in both the higher and lower pay grade groups, including handling work stress, attention to detail, persistence, and adaptability. On the other hand, three skills have nearly a 1 point jump in importance rating across the pay grade groups: decisionmaking, project planning, and written communication. Interestingly, skills such as "teamwork and team building" and "leading, motivating, and inspiring others" have very high importance even in the lower grades, as these skills are given the same high importance in the Army from the beginning of service.

APPENDIX B

Introduction to Task Lists for Army MOSs

As stated in Chapter Two, the O*NET database consists of a series of modules in six different content areas. The six that we administered to Army soldiers are reviewed in Chapter Two. Because none of these modules were job-specific, we were able to administer the surveys to soldiers in the exact form used for civilian occupations.

O*NET also produces occupation-specific modules for individual civilian jobs, and these modules may well have some importance for the Army. The module we consider in this appendix is the occupation-specific task list. These are widely used in the civilian sector for a variety of purposes, including to derive performance criteria for individual occupations. If the Army decides to expand the occupational analysis illustrated in this report to assist veterans in the search for employment, it may also want to produce task lists that are associated with individual MOSs, emphasizing the description of what soldiers do in terms understandable to civilian employers.

As part of this research, we undertook the production of task lists for MOSs 11B and 19K, and conducted a pilot test with 11B soldiers at JBLM. The task lists were designed for four purposes:

- provide descriptions of Army occupations in civilian terms
- help those analyzing the quantitative data on Army MOS identify outliers in cases where a soldier has a job outside his or her MOS
- provide the basis for further qualitative study of Army occupations and how they relate to civilian occupations
- determine how similar or different tasks are across MOS.

Procedure

In producing the tasks, we followed the spirit of the O*NET procedure in deriving tasks. Below, we list each of the O*NET stages and what we did to derive tasks for Army MOSs:

- Task Searching Stage
  - To identify the tasks required for each MOS, we used Army publication Pamphlet 611-21, the *MOS Smart Book*. Although this publication describes task by skill level, we endeavored to aggregate up to the level of the MOS as a whole. To complete our work, we broke down the descriptions into individual tasks; for example, we identified 69 separate tasks for 11B.
- Task Matching Stage
  - This stage requires that tasks in the subject occupation be compared to tasks in other occupations in an effort to standardize the task list across all occupations. In our case, we examined the tasks of police and first-line supervisors of police (and other occupations) in the civilian sector to serve as a guide in how to modify Army descriptions to be more in line with comparable tasks on the civilian side.
  - We also matched the tasks of MOS 19K with those of 11B, again endeavoring to standardize the language across occupations when dealing with the same task. Even when tasks were different, we sought to document very similar tasks with as few wording changes as possible.
- Task Sorting Stage
  - We first divided the task list from Army Pamphlet 611-21 into separate task statements and then numbered them. We then divided the numbered tasks into higher-level activities—shoot, move, communicate, assess, and lead were used for both MOSs—and grouped tasks by those categories.
- Task Writing Stage
  - Used similar wording when possible (see Task Matching Stage).
  - Combined similar tasks across skill levels.
  - Distinguished essential from secondary tasks.

  - Combined tasks where warranted.
- Task Revision Stage: In this stage, we re-reviewed our task list to ask the following questions:
  - Does this list of "essential" tasks adequately cover the occupation or should additional tasks be added?
  - Can we reduce the number of tasks by combining some or moving some to "secondary"?
  - Can we further simplify the language in some of the tasks?
  - What is the best order for the tasks for those taking the survey?
- Task Editing Stage
  - Edited the resulting revised task list to make sure they adequately represented MOSs 11B and 19K.

Task Lists

Table B.1 shows the task list we derived for 11B. Note that these are not all the tasks, just the primary ones. Secondary tasks were excluded because we wanted to maintain a similar level of detail to the task lists developed for civilian occupations.

To examine differences in civilian-oriented task descriptions among maneuver, fires, and effects occupations, we constructed a task list for one additional MOS, 19K, or M1 armor crewman. Table B.2 shows the primary task list derived for MOS 19K. The major finding was that, at this generic level, tasks were not much different between the two MOSs, even though the task lists in Army Pamphlet 611-21 were not always complete or simply used significantly different words. For example, "coordinates the evacuation of casualties" is listed under 19K but not in 11B. Or where 11B has a task for a gunner that is "detects, acquires, identifies and engages targets," 19K has "operates main gun controls or firing controls" and "fires main gun." At a higher level, both MOSs require the same tasks of shooting, moving, communicating, assessing, maintaining weapons and equipment, and leading. In our list, of the 16 tasks derived for 11B, 12 carried over word-for-word to 19K. The remaining four tasks were largely similar, although they required some rewording. Finally, one task (number 17) needed to be

Table B.1
Skill List Derived for MOS 11B Infantryman

1. Move mounted or dismounted, individually or as part of a team, to provide for public safety by maintaining order, responding to emergencies, protecting people, property or terrain/infrastructure. Locate and neutralize dangerous individuals using physical force and weapons systems according to defined procedures and rules of engagement.
2. Employ and maintain assigned weapons and equipment in normal and limited visibility.
3. Identify and assess threats, damage, and emergency-request information to determine response requirements.
4. Observe and report suspicious persons and situations, safety hazards, and unusual, threatening, or illegal activity.
5. Search and evaluate terrain and urban areas to exploit or remove physical security vulnerabilities; photograph or draw diagrams, question witnesses.
6. Navigate, mounted or dismounted, using a map or GPS assistance; familiar with movement techniques in limited visibility and darkness.
7. Operate/ drive assigned wheeled vehicle, or tracked vehicle in varied off road terrain, on highway, and in urban environments.
8. Record facts, prepare reports, and communicate them orally, over radio, in person, or in written text in order to document incidents and activities.
9. Relay complaint and emergency-request information orally to a subordinate, or via radio communications/text to appropriate dispatcher.
10. Operate and maintain radio communications equipment.
11. Receive and issue written and/or verbal orders and translate to the appropriate subordinate level of execution.
12. Supervise, direct, and lead teams to complete a task; coordinate efforts with other teams and report status of activities.
13. Develop and implement training programs to ensure compliance with established standards of performance for operations.
14. Inspect subordinates, assigned weapons, vehicles, equipment, and/or facilities to ensure their safe and effective functioning for operations.
15. Forecast requirements and supervise receipt, storage, and distribution of ammunition, supplies, and rations to subordinates.
16. Employ specified explosives and demolitions or engage in construction activities to breach, degrade, or destroy structures, roads, obstacles, or to improve protection/ fortification.

SOURCE: Derived from Army Pamphlet 611-21.

Table B.2
Skill List Derived for MOS 19K Armor Crewman

1. Move mounted as part of a vehicle crew, to provide for public safety by maintaining order, responding to emergencies, protecting people, property or terrain/infrastructure. Locate and neutralize dangerous individuals using physical force and weapons systems according to defined procedures and rules of engagement.
2. Employ and maintain assigned weapons and equipment in normal and limited visibility.
3. Identify and assess threats, damage, and emergency-request information to determine response requirements.
4. Observe and report suspicious persons and situations, safety hazards, and unusual, threatening, or illegal activity.
5. Search and evaluate terrain and urban areas to exploit or remove physical security vulnerabilities; photograph or draw diagrams, question witnesses.
6. Navigate, mounted or dismounted, using a map or GPS assistance; familiar with movement techniques in limited visibility and darkness.
7. Operate/ drive assigned wheeled vehicle, or tracked vehicle in varied off road terrain, on highway, and in urban environments.
8. Record facts, prepare reports, and communicate them orally, over radio, in person, or in written text in order to document incidents and activities.
9. Relay complaint and emergency-request information orally to a subordinate, or via radio communications/text to appropriate dispatcher.
10. Operate and maintain radio communications equipment.
11. Receive and issue visual, written and/or verbal orders and translate to the appropriate subordinate level of execution.
12. Supervise, direct, and lead teams to complete a task; coordinate efforts with other teams and report status of activities.
13. Develop and implement training programs to ensure compliance with established standards of performance for operations.
14. Inspect subordinates, assigned weapons, vehicles, equipment, and/or facilities to ensure their safe and effective functioning for operations.
15. Forecast requirements and supervise receipt, storage, and distribution of ammunition, supplies, maintenance and rations to subordinates.
16. Employ specified techniques and heavy machinery to breach, degrade, or destroy structures or obstacles or to improve protection/fortification.
17. Conduct operator-level vehicle maintenance of heavy machinery; assist in the recovery and towing of heavy machinery, assist mechanics in higher level maintenance and repair.

SOURCE: Derived from Army Pamphlet 611-21.

added for 19K. To make the differences easier to identify in Table B.2, we underlined in Table B.2 where the task description differed from what is shown in Table B.1.

Survey Results for MOS 11B

We tested the 11B task list on soldiers at JBLM, where we administered a separate questionnaire to 85 soldiers who identified themselves as 11B. We first asked the following question:

1. Which of the following best describes how closely the description in the shaded box matches the duties and responsibilities of your current position?

MOS 11B Infantryman
Supervises, leads, or serves as a member of an infantry activity that employs individual small arms weapons or heavy anti-armor crew served weapons, either vehicle or dismounted, in support of offensive and defensive combat operations.

(Check one)

- ☐ It describes almost exactly what I do.
- ☐ Most of it matches, but there are a few things that don't match what I do.
- ☐ Some things match, but most of it does not match what I do.
- ☐ It does not at all describe what I do

Of the 85 soldiers identifying as 11B, 78 indicated that the statement above described exactly or mostly what they do. For those, we asked them to indicate whether individual tasks were relevant (yes or no), and, if relevant, the frequency and importance of the individual tasks (Table A.3).

Frequency was defined on a 7-point scale as follows:

1. Once per year or less
2. More than once a year
3. More than once a month
4. More than once a week
5. Daily
6. Several times per day
7. Hourly or more often.

Importance was defined on a 5-point scale as follows:

1. Not important
2. Somewhat important
3. Important
4. Very important
5. Extremely important.

Table B.3 shows the average scores reported for each of the tasks reported by the 78 11Bs at JBLM. As can be seen, the responses validate the task list in that all tasks were identified as both important and undertaken frequently. The average frequency of undertaking tasks is between once a month and once a week for most tasks, with the exception of "teamwork," which happens more than daily, and "issuing orders" and "inspections," which can occur several times a day. Importance is uniformly high, typically between very important and extremely important, with "inspections" receiving the highest ratings, but occasionally a little bit lower (e.g., "search and evaluate terrain or urban areas").

There was also an open-ended question on the survey for respondents to fill in tasks they felt we missed. Fifteen soldiers made 30 total task suggestions. Some of the suggestions listed what we would identify more as KSAs or work attributes than tasks; for example, "remain flexible and adaptive in the face of ever-changing tasks and requirements," or "meet strict deadlines." Other questions seemed to advocate for more specificity in the task descriptions. For example, while task 13

Table B.3
Ratings for MOS 11B Infantryman

Task	Average Frequency	Average Importance
1. Move mounted or dismounted, individually or as part of a team, to provide for public safety by maintaining order, responding to emergencies, protecting people, property or terrain/infrastructure. Locate and neutralize dangerous individuals using physical force and weapons systems according to defined procedures and rules of engagement.	3.4	4.3
2. Employ and maintain assigned weapons and equipment in normal and limited visibility.	4.0	4.4
3. Identify and assess threats, damage, emergency-request information to determine response requirements.	3.5	4.1
4. Observe and report suspicious persons and situations, safety hazards, and unusual, threatening, or illegal activity.	3.2	3.9
5. Search and evaluate terrain and urban areas to exploit or remove physical security vulnerabilities; photograph or draw diagrams, question witnesses.	2.9	3.7
6. Navigate, mounted or dismounted, using a map or GPS assistance; familiar with movement techniques in limited visibility and darkness.	3.3	4.2
7. Operate/ drive assigned wheeled vehicle, or tracked vehicle in varied off road terrain, on highway, and in urban environments.	3.4	4.0
8. Record facts, prepare reports, and communicate them orally, over radio, in person, or in written text in order to document incidents and activities.	3.7	4.0
9. Relay complaint and emergency-request information orally to a subordinate, or via radio communications/text to appropriate dispatcher.	3.3	3.9
10. Operate and maintain radio communications equipment.	3.8	4.1
11. Receive and issue written and/or verbal orders and translate to the appropriate subordinate level of execution.	4.4	4.2
12. Supervise, direct, and lead teams to complete a task; coordinate efforts with other teams and report status of activities.	5.2	4.4
13. Develop and implement training programs to ensure compliance with established standards of performance for operations.	3.9	4.2

Table B.3—Continued

Task	Average Frequency	Average Importance
14. Inspect subordinates, assigned weapons, vehicles, equipment, and/or facilities to ensure their safe and effective functioning for operations.	4.4	4.6
15. Forecast requirements and supervise receipt, storage, and distribution of ammunition, supplies, and rations to subordinates	3.5	3.9

SOURCE: Derived from survey of responses of 78 11Bs at JBLM. Note that Q16 was added later to the task list, and not in time to be included in the survey.

is "develop and implement training programs . . . ," other suggestions were "conduct physical training" and "organize training events."

One suggested task that should be added to our list and which would actually apply broadly across MOSs was "counseling and mentoring soldiers." A related suggestion, "manage the health, welfare, and morale of 43 soldiers and their families" is a good suggestion for how soldiers can relay responsibilities in terms that are both highly specific and understandable in the civilian sector.

To be usable to veterans, civilian-oriented task lists would need to be created for all MOSs in the Army. This would require a focused Army effort; the examples above are meant to be illustrative as opposed to definitive as to what might be produced. The benefits of such an exercise could well go beyond helping veterans. For example, constructing such civilian-oriented task lists may be helpful in integrating the more technical tasks descriptions in Army publications across both MOSs and branches.

APPENDIX C

Additional Information on Occupation Surveys

In this appendix, we provide some additional information on our survey sample and analysis, including survey sample sizes by MOS and survey packet and measures of inter-rater reliability.

Sample Size

Table C.1 shows the number of survey packets completed by MOS. The first ten MOSs in the table (highlighted in green) had a sufficient sample size for analysis, i.e., at least eight responses to each survey packet. The remaining MOSs did not meet this threshold for at least one survey packet, so could not be included in our occupation analysis. However, some of these additional MOSs could potentially be analyzed if a few additional survey packets are completed.

Validation

Before we conducted our analysis to match Army MOSs with civilian occupations, we first wanted to determine whether soldiers were able to successfully and consistently identify attributes of their MOS. The most frequently used measure of inter-rater reliability is known as Fleiss's kappa (κ). Kappa is a measure of how well raters agree with one another. In the simplest case, where there are two raters choosing a dichotomous outcome, kappa is defined as the expected outcome (the percentage of matches due to chance) subtracted from the observed

Table C.1
Survey Sample by MOS and Survey Packet

MOS		Knowledge and Work Styles	Skills	Abilities	Work Activities	Work Context	Total
11B	Infantryman	36	36	38	33	35	178
12B	Combat engineer	24	24	15	16	18	97
13B	Cannon crewmember	8	9	9	9	9	44
19D	Cavalry scout	20	22	17	20	20	99
19K	M1 armor crewman	17	20	11	18	15	81
31B	Military police	16	15	12	18	20	81
35F	Intelligence analyst	8	8	9	8	10	43
68W	Health care specialist	19	17	12	20	17	85
91B	Wheeled vehicle mechanic	16	14	9	19	16	74
92Y	Unit supply specialist	9	10	8	9	9	45
11C	Indirect fire Infantryman	8	8	5	8	9	38
13F	Fire support specialist	8	8	5	8	9	38
25B	Information technology specialist	6	7	3	6	9	31
25U	Signal support systems specialist	7	9	7	5	6	34
42A	Human resources specialist	8	7	3	8	7	33

Table C.1—Continued

MOS		Knowledge and Work Styles	Skills	Abilities	Work Activities	Work Context	Total
74D	Chemical, biological, radiological and nuclear specialist	7	7	5	6	7	32
88M	Motor transport operator	9	12	2	10	12	45
92A	Automated logistical specialist	8	8	2	7	5	30
92F	Petroleum supply specialist	2	10	5	3	7	27
92G	Food service specialist	3	2	1	3	2	11
	Total	239	253	178	234	242	1,146

NOTE: We collected an additional 82 packets in MOSs not listed on this chart, for a total of 1,228 survey packets.

outcome. This number is bounded by –1 and 1, where positive values indicate that the raters agreed more often than chance would have predicted.

The standard interpretation of kappa is given by Landis and Koch (1977) in Table C.2. However, there is no empirical basis for this interpretation—it is correctly understood as a heuristic. Additionally there are reasons to believe that the interpretation of kappa differs in different contexts. Kappa is likely to be lower when there are a large number of categories (in our case, we have 5- and 7-point scales), when there are a large number of dimensions to assess (in our case there are sometimes 50 or more assessment questions being answered), or when there is a large baseline agreement (when everyone is nearly certain that one or two outcomes will never occur), then the expected outcome is high, making it more difficult to achieve a high kappa.

Table C.2
Interpretation of Fleiss's Kappa

K	Interpretation
< 0	Poor agreement
0.01–0.20	Slight agreement
0.21–0.40	Fair agreement
0.41–0.60	Moderate agreement
0.61–0.80	Substantial agreement
0.81–1.00	Almost perfect agreement

SOURCE: Landis and Kotch, 1977.

Additionally, there are some particular reasons why we are wary of using kappa as a measure of inter-rater reliability in our study. The most important reason is that soldiers are not objectively appraising the same MOS, rather they are assessing the MOS based on the tasks they perform when they do the job. Since there is a considerable amount of task heterogeneity within an MOS, it is likely that our inter-rater reliability will be low. Secondly, primary duties within the MOS change as soldiers gain experience and are promoted. Finally, some soldiers will be making an assessment based on their duties while in garrison, while others may be assessing their duties after being recently deployed. We administered the questionnaire to soldiers of pay grades E2–E9 and initially calculated kappa across all ranks.

Tables C.3 and C.4 show our calculations of kappa for each MOS and O*NET module (KSAs, work activities, work contexts, and work styles). Recall that for the modules shown in Table C.3, there are two parts for each question, an importance (IM, on a 5-point scale) and a level (LV, on a 7-point scale). We calculate kappa separately for each part. Additionally, we provide the average score across all modules. Modules shown in Table C.4 each have single-part question on a 5-point scale. For the most part, the average kappa scores in Table C.3 are in the 0.2–0.4 range, indicating "fair" reliability for six out of ten MOSs. The other four MOS ranged from 0.15–0.18, thus just miss-

Table C.3
K Values by MOS for Survey Modules with Two-Part Questions

	Knowledge		Skills		Abilities		Work Activities		
MOS	IM	LV	IM	LV	IM	LV	IM	LV	Average
11B	0.21	0.23	0.29	0.25	0.15	0.20	0.17	0.16	0.21
12B	0.20	0.22	0.23	0.19	0.07	0.08	0.10	0.08	0.15
13B	0.28	0.23	0.42	0.31	0.06	0.05	0.04	0.03	0.18
19D	0.25	0.22	0.17	0.15	0.09	0.18	0.15	0.14	0.17
19K	0.39	0.35	0.29	0.23	0.13	0.25	0.14	0.14	0.24
31B	0.38	0.36	0.28	0.20	0.07	0.10	0.12	0.11	0.20
35F	0.40	0.41	0.26	0.15	0.44	0.29	0.23	0.24	0.30
68W	0.34	0.39	0.37	0.38	0.05	0.04	0.16	0.19	0.24
91B	0.27	0.23	0.30	0.20	0.07	0.08	0.18	0.14	0.18
92Y	0.42	0.41	0.34	0.33	0.24	0.15	0.24	0.17	0.29

NOTE: Importance (IM) is rated on a 5-point scale; level (LV) is rated on a 7-point scale.

ing the cutoff for fair, with combat engineers (12B) having the lowest measure of inter-rater reliability. Given that we asked soldiers to use their own experience when filling out the O*NET questionnaire, it is not surprising that the level of inter-rater reliability is low. Soldiers who completed the surveys varied by years of service, pay grade, number and duration of deployments, and skill level. Of particular concern are the abilities and work activities modules for the combat engineers (12B) and cannon crewmembers (13B). In these cases, inter-rater reliability were sometimes less than 0.10, suggesting that soldiers in those MOSs have considerably different experiences of their day-to-day tasks.

In Table C.4, the measures of kappa are considerably higher, particularly for the work context module. In part this is occurring because each question is measured on a single 5-point scale. Additionally, these questions focus more on job characteristics than on the soldier's characteristics. For each MOS, the average score in Table C.4 is higher than

Table C.4
K Values by MOS for Survey Modules with Single-Part Questions

MOS	Work Context	Work Styles	Average
11B	0.33	0.14	0.23
12B	0.32	0.08	0.20
13B	0.27	0.21	0.24
19D	0.34	0.11	0.22
19K	0.29	0.18	0.23
31B	0.34	0.16	0.25
35F	0.51	0.30	0.40
68W	0.35	0.11	0.23
91B	0.42	0.06	0.24
92Y	0.50	0.30	0.40

NOTE: These surveys contain single-part questions on a 5-point scale.

0.20, indicating "fair" agreement. In a few cases, kappa scores are 0.40, right at the cusp of "moderate" agreement (intelligence analyst [35F] and unit supply specialist [92Y]).

A second way of utilizing kappa is to look at the MOSs with the highest and lowest averages, as a way of gauging the heterogeneity of the MOS. When we average kappa scores across all six modules (not shown), we find that all the MOSs with average scores below the 0.20 cutoff of "fair" agreement are maneuver, fires, and effects MOSs: combat engineer (12B), cannon crewmember (13B), and cavalry scout (19D). While wheeled vehicle repairers (91B) had a low score on the first four modules in Table D.3, their average increased once we include the work context and work styles modules.

Reliability Analysis for MOS 11B (Infantryman) by Pay Grade

Since we have a relatively large sample of surveys from MOS 11B, we conducted a separate reliability assessment for junior (pay grades

E1–E4) and senior (pay grades E-5 and above) enlisted personnel. Table C.5 compares the inter-rater reliability results (κ) for the entire sample with the subgroups of E1–E4 and E5–E9. We find that kappa increases when we calculate it separately for junior and senior enlisted personnel. We interpret this as evidence of job heterogeneity by rank. Given a sufficient number of observations, we could conceivably conduct a separate occupation analysis for every pay grade within an MOS and provide more tailored lists of high-quality military-civilian job matches.

Table C.5
κ Values by Pay Grade Group for MOS 11B (Infantrymen)

Pay Grades	Skills		Knowledge		Work Activities		Abilities		Work Styles	Work Context	Average
	IM	LV	IM	LV	IM	LV	IM	LV	IM	IM	
All	0.29	0.25	0.21	0.23	0.17	0.16	0.15	0.20	0.14	0.33	0.21
E1–E4	0.26	0.22	0.21	0.23	0.16	0.14	0.44	0.45	0.14	0.30	0.26
E5–E9	0.44	0.36	0.22	0.27	0.29	0.29	0.12	0.18	0.11	0.48	0.28

APPENDIX D

Additional Military-Civilian Occupation Matches

Table D.1 lists all the civilian occupations that are high-quality matches for four or more of the ten MOSs we analyzed.

Table D.1
High-Quality Civilian Occupation Matches with Four or More Army MOSs

Civilian Occupation	Number of U.S. Jobs	Median Wages	Education Required at Entry	Number of MOS Matches
Aircraft cargo handling supervisors	5,750	$47,760	High school diploma	8
Aircraft mechanics and service technicians	116,830	$56,990	Postsecondary certification	8
Automotive service technicians and mechanics	633,390	$37,120	Postsecondary certification	6
Boilermakers	17,210	$59,860	High school diploma	5
Bus and truck mechanics and diesel engine specialists	243,080	$43,630	High school diploma	4
Captains, mates, and pilots of water vessels	30,690	$72,340	Postsecondary certification	9
Chemical equipment operators and tenders	64,710	$48,090	High school diploma	5
Chemical plant and system operators	37,490	$55,900	High school diploma	5
Commercial pilots	38,170	$75,620	Postsecondary certification	4

Table D.1—Continued

Civilian Occupation	Number of U.S. Jobs	Median Wages	Education Required at Entry	Number of MOS Matches
Construction and related workers, all other	31,190	$35,400	High school diploma	4
Continuous mining machine operators	11,540	$48,440	Less than high school	4
Correctional officers and jailers	434,420	$39,780	High school diploma	5
Crushing, grinding, and polishing machine setters, operators, and tenders	29,980	$33,070	High school diploma	5
Derrick operators, oil and gas	20,760	$48,410	Less than high school	4
Detectives and criminal investigators	108,720	$79,870	High school diploma	5
Electrical and electronics repairers, commercial and industrial equipment	65,900	$54,640	Associate's degree	4
Electrical and electronics repairers, powerhouse, substation, and relay	22,120	$71,400	Postsecondary certification	5
Electricians	566,930	$51,110	Postsecondary certification	4
Electronic equipment installers and repairers, motor vehicles	11,460	$31,020	Postsecondary certification	4
Electronic home entertainment equipment installers and repairers	26,590	$36,090	Postsecondary certification	4
Emergency medical technicians and paramedics	235,760	$31,700	Postsecondary certification	5
Explosives workers, ordnance handling experts, and blasters	7,970	$52,140	High school diploma	5
Fire inspectors and investigators	11,370	$56,130	Some college	9
Firefighters	308,790	$45,970	High school diploma	9
First-line supervisors of construction trades and extraction workers	496,370	$60,990	High school diploma	7

Table D.1—Continued

Civilian Occupation	Number of U.S. Jobs	Median Wages	Education Required at Entry	Number of MOS Matches
First-line supervisors of correctional officers	45,150	$57,970	High school diploma	4
First-line supervisors of farming, fishing, and forestry workers	18,530	$44,880	High school diploma	8
First-line supervisors of fire fighting and prevention workers	59,870	$70,670	High school diploma	10
First-line supervisors of helpers, laborers, and material movers, hand	171,720	$46,690	High school diploma	8
First-line supervisors of landscaping, lawn service, and groundskeeping workers	101,190	$43,160	High school diploma	5
First-line supervisors of mechanics, installers, and repairers	434,810	$62,150	High school diploma	9
First-line supervisors of police and detectives	101,420	$80,930	High school diploma	6
First-line supervisors of production and operating workers	592,830	$55,520	High school diploma	7
First-line supervisors of transportation and material-moving machine and vehicle operators	197,000	$54,930	High school diploma	6
Food service managers	198,610	$48,560	Less than high school	6
Forest and conservation technicians	30,310	$35,260	High school diploma	7
Gas plant operators	16,320	$64,100	High school diploma	4
Hazardous materials removal workers	42,250	$38,520	High school diploma	5
Heating, air conditioning, and refrigeration mechanics and installers	261,390	$44,630	Postsecondary certification	6
Highway maintenance workers	140,650	$36,580	High school diploma	4

Table D.1—Continued

Civilian Occupation	Number of U.S. Jobs	Median Wages	Education Required at Entry	Number of MOS Matches
Installation, maintenance, and repair workers, all other	138,460	$37,220	High school diploma	4
Licensed practical and licensed vocational nurses	695,610	$42,490	Postsecondary certification	4
Manufactured building and mobile home installers	3,280	$29,600	Less than high school	7
Millwrights	39,290	$50,460	High school diploma	7
Motorboat operators	4,060	$37,120	Postsecondary certification	6
Petroleum pump system operators, refinery operators, and gaugers	41,700	$62,830	High school diploma	5
Plant and system operators, all other	11,610	$55,230	High school diploma	5
Plumbers, pipefitters, and steamfitters	372,570	$50,660	Postsecondary certification	4
Police and sheriff's patrol officers	638,810	$56,810	High school diploma	7
Radiation therapists	16,380	$80,090	Associate's degree	4
Rail yard engineers, dinkey operators, and hostlers	3,900	$43,880	High school diploma	5
Registered nurses	2,687,310	$66,640	Associate's degree	4
Respiratory therapists	119,410	$56,730	Associate's degree	4
Respiratory therapy technicians	10,610	$47,810	Associate's degree	4
Rotary drill operators, oil and gas	26,480	$53,160	Less than high school	4
Separating, filtering, clarifying, precipitating, and still machine setters, operators, and tenders	43,310	$38,590	High school diploma	4

Table D.1—Continued

Civilian Occupation	Number of U.S. Jobs	Median Wages	Education Required at Entry	Number of MOS Matches
Septic tank servicers and sewer pipe cleaners	24,350	$34,810	Less than high school	8
Service unit operators, oil, gas, and mining	62,080	$44,970	High school diploma	5
Sheet metal workers	132,530	$45,070	High school diploma	4
Ship engineers	10,060	$68,100	Postsecondary certification	10
Signal and track switch repairers	7,880	$60,640	Associate's degree	4
Structural iron and steel workers	60,010	$48,200	High school diploma	5
Telecommunications equipment installers and repairers, except line installers	213,620	$55,190	Postsecondary certification	7
Transportation inspectors	24,350	$69,170	Postsecondary certification	7
Water and wastewater treatment plant and system operators	111,640	$44,100	High school diploma	4
Wind turbine service technicians	3,710	$48,800	High school diploma	4

Lists of Figures and Tables

Figure

Tables

Abbreviations

AC	active component
FY	fiscal year
JBLM	Joint Base Lewis-McChord
KSAs	knowledge, skills, and abilities
MOS	military occupational specialty
O*NET	Occupational Information Network
RC	reserve component
RN	registered nurse
SOC	standard occupation classification

References

Alexopoulos, Michelle, and Tricia Gladden (2004). "The Effects of Wealth and Unemployment Benefits on Search Behavior and Labor Market Transitions," Working Paper, University of Toronto Department of Economics, Toronto, Canada.

Blackaby, David H., Paul L. Latreille, Philip D. Murphy, Nigel C. O'Leary, and Peter J. Sloane (2007). "An Analysis of Reservation Wages for the Economically Inactive," *Economics Letters*, Vol. 97, No. 1, pp. 1–5.

Bloemen, Hans G., and Elena G. F. Stancanelli (2001). "Individual Wealth, Reservation Wages, and Transitions into Employment," *Journal of Labor Economics*, Vol. 19, No. 2, pp. 400–439.

Brown, Sarah, Roberts, Jennifer, and Karl Taylor (2010). "Reservation Wages, Labour Market Participation and Health," *Journal of the Royal Statistical Society, Series A: Statistics in Society*, Vol. 173, No. 3, pp. 501–529.

Bureau of Labor Statistics (March 11, 2010). "Standard Occupational Classification: 53-4031 Railroad Conductors and Yardmasters." As of September 30, 2016:
http://www.bls.gov/soc/2010/soc534031.htm

——— (September 2, 2016). *The Employment Situation—August 2016*, Washington, D.C. As of September 29, 2016:
http://www.bls.gov/news.release/pdf/empsit.pdf

Burdett, Kenneth (1979). "Unemployment Insurance Payments as a Search Subsidy: A Theoretical Analysis," *Economic Inquiry*, Vol. 17, No. 3, pp. 333–343.

Burdett, Kenneth, and Dale Mortensen (1980). "Search, Layoffs, and Labor Market Equilibrium," *Journal of Political Economy*, Vol. 88, No. 4, pp. 652–672.

Burdett, Kenneth, and Tara Vishwanath (1988). "Reservation Wages and Learning," *Review of Economic Studies*, Vol. 55, No. 4, pp. 655–665.

Danforth, John P. (1979). "On the Role of Consumption and Decreasing Absolute Risk Aversion in the Theory of Job Search," in Steven A. Lippman and John J. McCall, eds., *Studies in the Economics of Search*, Amsterdam: North Holland, pp. 109–131.

DellaVigna, Stefano, and M. Daniele Paserman (2005). "Job Search and Impatience," *Journal of Labor Economics*, Vol. 23, No. 3, pp. 527–588.

Department of the Army (2008a). *MOS Smart Book*, Pamphlet 611-21, Washington, D.C. As of November 30, 2015:
http://usacac.army.mil/cac2/Retention/mos%20book.doc

——— (September 2008b). *Soldier's Manual of Common Tasks: Warrior Leader Skills Level 2, 3, and 4*, STP 21-24-SMCT, Washington, D.C. As of May 3, 2016:
https://armypubs.us.army.mil/doctrine/DR_pubs/dr_aa/pdf/stp21_24.pdf

——— (August 2015). *Soldier's Manual of Common Tasks: Warrior Skills Level 1*, STP 21-1-SMCT, Washington, D.C. As of May 3, 2016:
https://armypubs.us.army.mil/doctrine/DR_pubs/dr_aa/pdf/stp21_1.pdf

Department of Defense Instruction 1322.29 (January 24, 2014). *Job Training, Employment Skills Training, Apprenticeships, and Internships (JTEST-AI) for Eligible Service Members*, Washington, D.C.: U.S. Department of Defense. As of September 27, 2016:
http://www.dtic.mil/whs/directives/corres/pdf/132229p.pdf

Flinn, Christopher J., and James J. Heckman (1982). "New Methods for Analyzing Structural Models of Labor Force Dynamics," *Journal of Econometrics*, Vol. 18, No. 1, pp. 115–168.

Gorter, Dirk, and Cees Gorter (1993). "The Relation between Unemployment Benefits, the Reservation Wage, and Search Duration," *Oxford Bulletin of Economics and Statistics*, Vol. 55, No. 2, pp. 199–214.

Gronau, Reuben (1971). "Information and Frictional Unemployment," *American Economic Review*, Vol. 61, No. 3, Part 1, pp. 290–301.

Hardison, Chaitra, Michael G. Shanley, Anna Rosefsky Saavedra, James C. Crowley, Jonathan P. Wong, and Paul S. Steinberg (2015). *What Veterans Bring to Civilian Workplaces: A Prototype Toolkit for Helping Private-Sector Employers Understand the Nontechnical Skills Taught in the Military*, Santa Monica, Calif.: RAND Corporation, TL-160-OSD. As of September 27, 2016:
http://www.rand.org/pubs/tools/TL160.html

Haurin, Donald R., and Kala S. Sridhar (2003). "The Impact of Local Unemployment Rates on Reservation Wages and the Duration of Search for a Job," *Applied Economics*, Vol. 35, No. 13, pp. 1469–1476.

Heaton, Paul, and Heather Krull (2012). *Unemployment Among Post-9/11 Veterans and Military Spouses After the Economic Downturn*, Santa Monica, Calif.: RAND Corporation, OP-376-OSD. As of September 27, 2016: http://www.rand.org/pubs/occasional_papers/OP376.html

Hogan, Vincent (2004). "Wage Aspirations and Unemployment Persistence," *Journal of Monetary Economics*, Vol. 51, No. 8, pp. 1623–1643.

Holzer, Harry J. (1986). "Reservation Wages and Their Labor Market Effects for Black and White Male Youth," *Journal of Human Resources*, Vol. 21, No. 2, pp. 157–177.

Jones, Stephen R. G. (1989). "Reservation Wages and the Cost of Unemployment," *Economica*, New Series, Vol. 56, No. 222, pp. 225–246.

Kasper, Hirschel (1967). "The Asking Price of Labor and the Duration of Unemployment," *Review of Economics and Statistics*, Vol. 49, No. 2, pp. 165–172.

Kiefer, Nicholas M., and George R. Neumann (1979). "An Empirical Job-Search Model, with a Test of the Constant Reservation-Wage Hypothesis," *Journal of Political Economy*, Vol. 87, No. 1, pp. 89–107.

Landis, J. R., and G. G. Koch (1977). "The Measurement of Observer Agreement for Categorical Data," *Biometrics*, Vol. 33, pp. 159–174.

Loughran, David S. (2014). *Why Is Veteran Unemployment So High?* Santa Monica, Calif.: RAND Corporation, RR-284-OSD, 2014. As of September 27, 2016: http://www.rand.org/pubs/research_reports/RR284.html

Lippman, Steven, and John J. McCall (1976). "Job Search in a Dynamic Economy," *Journal of Economic Theory*, Vol. 12, No. 3, pp. 365–390.

Mariani, Matthew (1999). "Replace with a Database: O*NET Replaces the Dictionary of Occupational Titles," *Occupational Outlook Quarterly*, Spring 1999. As of September 30, 2016: http://www.bls.gov/careeroutlook/1999/Spring/art01.pdf

McCall, Brian P. (1994). "The Effect of Job Heterogeneity on Reservation Wages," *International Economic Review*, Vol. 35, No. 3, pp. 773–791.

McCall, John J. (1970). "Economics of Information and Job Search," *Quarterly Journal of Economics*, Vol. 84, No. 1, pp. 113–126.

Mitra, Sophie (2007). "The Reservation Wages of Social Security Disability Insurance Beneficiaries," *Social Security Bulletin*, Vol. 67, No. 4, pp. 89–111.

Mortensen, Dale T. (1970). "Job Search, the Duration of Unemployment, and the Phillips Curve," *American Economic Review*, Vol. 60, No. 5, pp. 847–862.

——— (1977). "Unemployment Insurance and Job Search Decisions," *Industrial and Labor Relations Review*, Vol. 30, No. 4, pp. 505–517.

——— (1986). "Job Search and Labor Market Analysis," in Orley Ashenfelter and Richard Layard, eds., *Handbook of Labor Economics*, Vol. 2, pp. 849–919. Amsterdam: North Holland.

O*NET Resource Center (undated). "The O*NET® Content Model," web page. As of September 27, 2016:
https://www.onetcenter.org/content.html

Petrongolo, Barbara, and Christopher Pissarides (2006). "Scale Effects in Markets with Search," *The Economic Journal*, Vol. 116, No. 508, pp. 21–44.

Petterson, Stephen M. (1997). "Are Young Black Men really less willing to Work?" *American Sociological Review*, Vol. 62, No. 4, pp. 605–613.

——— (1998). "Black-White Differences in Reservation Wages and Joblessness: A Replication," *Journal of Human Resources*, Vol. 33, No. 3, pp. 758–770.

Public Law 101-510 (1990). National Defense Authorization Act for Fiscal Year 1991, Section 502(a)(1), 104 Stat. 1485, 1551.

Russell, T. L., M. D. Mumford, and N. G. Peterson (1996). *Applicability of the Department of Labor's O*NET for Army Occupational Analysis*, Alexandria, Va., ARI Research Note 96-68.

Russell, T. L., A. Sinclair, J. Erdheim, M. Ingerick, K. Owens, N. Peterson, et al. (2008). *Evaluating the O*NET Occupational Analysis System for Army Competency Development*, Contract for Manpower, Personnel, Leader Development, and Training for the U.S. Army Research Institute, Alexandria, Va.: HumRRO.

Salop, S. C. (1973). "Systematic Job Search and Unemployment," *Review of Economic Studies*, Vol. 40, No. 2, pp. 191–201.

Sant, Donald T. (1977). "Reservation Wage Rules and Learning Behavior," *Review of Economics and Statistics*, Vol. 59, No. 1, pp. 43–49.

Stern, Steven (1989). "Estimating a Simultaneous Search Model," *Journal of Labor Economics*, Vol. 7, No. 3, pp. 348–369.

Tan, Michelle (June 10, 2015). "Army Lays Out Plan to Cut 40,000 Soldiers," *Army Times*. As of November 2, 2015:
http://www.armytimes.com/story/military/pentagon/2015/07/09/army-outlines-40000-cuts/29923339/

Van den Berg, Gerard J. (1990). "Nonstationarity in Job Search Theory," *Review of Economic Studies*, Vol. 57, No. 2, pp. 255–277.

Wolpin, Kenneth I. (1987). "Estimating a Structural Search Model: The Transition from School to Work," *Econometrica*, Vol. 55, No. 4, pp. 801–817.